Star Turns

Tim Walker

In memory of the last of the Mawby Triplets (1922–2012)

Star Turns

Tim Walker

SunRise

SunRise

First published in Great Britain in 2021 by SunRise

SunRise Publishing Ltd
Kemp House
152–160 City Road
London EC1V 2NX

ISBN 978-1-914489-00-6

A CIP catalogue record for this book is available from the British Library.

Typeset in Bookman Old Style, titles in Impact, captions in Acumin.

Printed by Kingsbury Press, Doncaster, England.

Contents

Foreword

Stardom is a fragile and possibly preposterous state of being. 'Not a profession,' as Lauren Bacall once noted, 'but an accident.' To her fellow actor, Fredric March, it was 'just an uneasy seat on top of a tricky toboggan'. A character in a novel by H G Wells probably put it best when he talked about this kind of success as 'a vulgar, tawdry, irksome, envied thing'.

In this book, which has been more than thirty years in the making, I write of seventy-one individuals who have had their own experiences of it.

There are those who have attained it, take it desperately seriously and try to cling on to it at all costs. It gives their lives meaning, and fills for them, I fancy, a spiritual emptiness. Some grasp its ironies, but have, often reluctantly, come to an accommodation with it. There are those who try to use it as a force for good, and others — sometimes — for vengeance. One or two have, with varying degrees of regret, seen it slip though their fingers. Others — and, tellingly, these tend to be women — reckon it comes at too high a price and have decided they'd be better off without it.

It's bestowed randomly, sometimes justly, sometimes unjustly, and can never be taken for granted. I think of all the young actors that never got to shine when the pandemic plunged theatres across the world into darkness. I commiserated with a few: some felt embittered, others could let the dream go. They recognised stardom would not necessarily have made their lives better, only different.

For all that, the question I still get asked, whenever I come back from an interview with a star, is: 'What's he/she like?' The word 'like' is an interesting one: it contains an expectation that there has to be something special. It's as if we can't accept that stars can be just like everyone else. Sometimes, however, I'm afraid they are: Rowan Atkinson, for instance, apologised to me profusely for being so dull. So did Sir Michael Hordern, though, in his case, he wasn't, not remotely.

There's a line in John Logan's play *Peter and Alice* that encapsulates this, when one of the characters observes: 'Famous people shouldn't be tiny, it seems dishonest.'

Star Turns is, inevitably, about human nature as much as it is about stardom. It says something, too, about how our society has changed since the mid-eighties — when I did the first interviews — to today. Maybe we've all grown up a bit over the years: we seem less het up now, for instance, about sex; more het up, maybe, about politics and identity.

I've written it in the spirit of the late critic Kenneth Tynan's *Profiles* — it's even inspired the cover design — and, I guess, as with that book, it says as much about the author as it does the subjects. Clever questions and fine writing are well and good, but all I hope that people will say of me when they read this is that I was fair: that I had the ones I liked and the ones I didn't like and I put them into these two categories with infinite care.

As this book goes to press, I turn my attention to *Star Turns: The Sequel*, which will broaden the definition of the word 'star' to include politicians. If you believe that Westminster and Capitol Hill is show business for ugly people, it may not be so very different.

Tim Walker, London, July 2021.

Publisher's Note

Early in 2021 we began the search for a good political book by contacting writers who, we thought, might capture the zeitgeist of our turbulent times. We knew that Tim Walker had emerged from the Twittersphere as a voice that could neatly skewer the fallacies and outright lies of our leaders, and we knew also that he had written for many of the great newspapers as well as producing a biography of Norma Major. I had previously exchanged emails with him and now asked, tentatively, if he had thought of writing another book. Yes, came the reply, but he was also thinking of weaving together the many interviews which had appeared in his *Star Turns* column in *The New European.* As soon as we began to read them, we realised these pieces were solid gold. It wasn't just the names that glittered (although they were impressive enough): it was the insights, the humour, and the exquisite style that made them jump off the page.

Pen portraits of the famous are harder to write than most imagine. I had once been a journalist, occasionally tasked with the celebrity interviews that other hacks had refused. I understood, only too well, the challenges: overbearing PR people, forbidden topics and ill-tempered subjects who view all press as the enemy. I also knew that — contrary to popular belief — actors can sometimes be shy, under-confident people who have never entirely come to terms with their own characters, in contrast to the ones they play on stage or screen. There were many late afternoons when I found myself staring at a blank screen, wondering how on earth I would get a thousand words out of the uncomfortable hour I'd just spent with a household name.

Tim consistently does more than sprinkle a little star dust into our lives. Time and again he crystallises what others might have sensed but not articulated, casting light into previously unseen corners of the lives we thought we knew. Best of all is his economy: he achieves, in a handful of words, what others might not have accomplished in a tome.

One of the most revealing pieces is an homage to his mother, Claudine Mawby. She was the last of the Mawby Triplets — an acting trio so famous their handprints were set in cement outside Grauman's Chinese Theatre in Hollywood. He records how she was a uniquely free spirit with little or no respect for authority who was brutally honest in her opinions and an unerringly good judge of character. Fortunately for us, she clearly gifted those talents to her son.

Here you have seventy-one of the world's most celebrated people captured by a master craftsman who analyses and defines but is never overawed. You will, at turns, be entertained, enlightened, surprised and occasionally shocked but, best of all, repeatedly made to laugh aloud at the wit, passion, talent and foibles of those who have entertained us for most of our lives (and a few who haven't).

We are especially grateful to Matt Kelly of *The New European* for allowing us to reproduce these stories.

Malcolm Turner, London, July 2021.

Lauren Bacall

L auren Bacall's publicist was adamant that the star would talk to me about any subject under the sun, except her first husband, Humphrey Bogart. 'She feels she's talked about him quite enough,' he said. 'So, I'd be obliged if you didn't mention him at all...'

Even as she was taking her seat beside me at Le Caprice, the fashionable St James's restaurant, it was his nickname that was first to cross her lips. 'Bogey and I used to come to this joint after the war, not long after it'd been established. He was very particular about where he ate, and, in London in those days, frankly, there wasn't a lot of choice.'

Bacall's second husband Jason Robards, whom it was generally reckoned she'd married on account of the fact he looked very much like her first husband, wearily called her 'the Widow Bogart'. After eight years and endless re-runs of old Bogart-Bacall classics like *The Big Sleep* and *Key Largo*, Robards, drinking heavily, realised she was never going to let him go and their marriage ended. Paul Dehn, who wrote the script to the 1974 film version of *Murder on the Orient Express*, was almost certainly making an in-joke when he had Bacall's character droning on incessantly about her former husband.

Bogart had died of cancer in 1957, when Bacall had been just thirty-two. My interview with her took place thirty years on, when she was making a now forgotten British thriller called *Tree of Hands*. It was clearly her publicist — rather than her — who yearned for her to change the record. 'Bogey understood what it was to be a man in a way most men nowadays don't,' Bacall said. 'He loved the outdoors, the sea, horses, all of that kind of stuff, but he also got that a real man could let a woman be a woman...'

She was wearing impenetrable sunglasses, which made it difficult to work out what she was thinking, and, certainly to start with, she was a lot more interested in the menu than me. 'Interviews are like blind dates,' she said, not looking up. 'You never

Lauren Bacall was married to Humphrey Bogart (twenty-four years her senior) from 1945 until his death in 1957.

know who the hell you're going to end up with, so the one thing I always insist upon is choosing the restaurant. The conversation may be boring, but at least that way I can ensure I get a decent meal.'

I was barely twenty-five, a Fleet Street newcomer just up from local newspapers, and I should probably have approached the lunch a lot more reverentially, but there were moments when it seemed to border on parody. We were, of course, seated at the restaurant's coveted corner table, and, at one point, Melvyn Bragg came up to pay homage. 'How lovely to see you. What are you doing?' The exchange of two 'mwaaah, mwaaah' kisses and then a laconic: 'Oh, a godawful movie, darling.'

Bacall understood that the retention of stardom required continual vigilance. A picture a newspaper used of her was every bit as important — if not more so — than the accompanying words, and she'd vetoed me bringing along a photographer lest it result in a study that was a little too candid. So, she'd brought along few snaps of her own. She was then in her mid-sixties and looking good, but none of the ones she pressed into my hands could have been fewer than ten years old.

The piece I wrote afterwards was not as kind as it perhaps should have been, but I realise now that it was the intensity of the love she had for Bogart that made the rest of her life so challenging and made her sometimes a bit of a prima donna. She'd suggested we meet again the next time she was in London. *The Observer*'s picture editor did for that: he deliberately chose the worst stock photo of her he could find.

Still, the day I lunched with Bacall was nevertheless the beginning of one enduring love affair in my life. And that was with Le Caprice.

Lauren Bacall was born in Brooklyn, New York, on 16 September 1924, and died in Manhattan, New York, on 12 August 2014, at the age of eighty-nine.

Ronnie Corbett

This is going to take a bit of explaining, but it was *The Winslow Boy* that introduced me to Ronnie Corbett. The late, great actor and comedian never appeared in the play, but his old friend Edward Hardwicke had, at the Chichester Festival Theatre in 2001. It was a wonderful production, and, if there had been any justice in the world, it should have transferred to London.

Some twelve years on, Terence Rattigan's play was revived at the Old Vic, with Henry Goodman playing the part of the father determined to fight for justice for his son. He wasn't a patch on Hardwicke and I said as much when I reviewed it. A few days later, I received a beautifully handwritten letter from Corbett, in which he said how thrilled he was that Hardwicke's portrayal had meant so much to me. Corbett explained that Hardwicke, who had died two years earlier, had been his best friend since they did their national service together as pilot officers in the RAF. Hardwicke had given the role everything he had, not least because his father, Sir Cedric Hardwicke, had previously played it in the classic 1948 film version, so it was for him — as Corbett put it — a matter of 'family pride'.

Corbett was then eighty-three, but full of life and enthusiasm. Afterwards, if I wrote a piece he disagreed with, he was on the phone. He never wanted an argument: he just wanted to establish why I had thought something. His silences could be damning. He had a strong sense of the power of words and of right and wrong.

Ronnie Corbett with trademark tartan trousers.

Around that time I had agreed — as a stunt to raise money for charity, rather than any obvious typecasting — to appear in a production of *Spamalot* at the Playhouse theatre. I was to play God. I told Corbett it would almost certainly be embarrassingly bad, but invited him along anyway. To my delight, he showed up on a cold, dank winter's night in a cheery tartan jacket and mauve waistcoat and was the life and soul of the after-party.

Corbett was, of course, a living legend, best known for appearing in the hugely successful BBC television series *The Two Ronnies* with his old friend Ronnie Barker, but also a string of films, such as the first *Casino Royale* and *No Sex Please, We're British* and the television sitcom *Sorry!* He'd also trodden the boards and done his share of pantos. He never, however, acted like a star: he was just interested in people, liked to laugh and wanted to make sure everyone around him was having a good time.

Not long afterwards, Corbett attended a gathering at 10 Downing Street hosted by David Cameron, when he was still prime minister. Corbett confided in me he didn't find Cameron at all impressive — 'too eager to please' — but, born in Edinburgh and a staunch defender of the Union, he was one of 200 public figures who subsequently signed an open letter expressing the hope that Scotland would vote to remain part of the United Kingdom in the independence referendum.

Presciently, Corbett sensed the storm clouds gathering over our country. It worried him that young people in particular seemed oblivious. Corbett had an understated sense of patriotism based on the idea that everyone should have the same chances in life he'd had. Childhood memories of the war had left him with a sense, too, of the fragility of freedom.

Our later conversations invariably ended with us both saying we must have lunch, but that was never to happen. Sometimes he would commit to a date, but later cancel, saying he was feeling 'a wee bit under the weather'. Over the months, our telephone calls became less frequent, and, when I phoned, I found myself talking more often than not to his wife, Annie. She was initially mystified why suddenly he seemed so weary. She was obviously worried sick about him, but she never once complained.

The Corbetts sought medical advice and motor neurone disease was diagnosed; a cruel and debilitating disease of the nervous system. Rumours began appearing in some tabloid newspapers about Corbett's health, but the couple had decided they would handle the ramifications themselves and in their own way. I've no doubt at all that Corbett, who had devoted his entire life to making people laugh, had been loath to make them sad. He died in the spring of 2016: I associate the moment now with a loss of innocence and the start of a harsher — and certainly less humorous — era.

Ronnie Corbett was born in Edinburgh, Scotland, on 4 December 1930, and died in Shirley, London, on 31 March 2016. He was eighty-five.

Patrick Kielty

When he was sixteen, Patrick Kielty's father, Jack, was shot six times by the loyalist Ulster Freedom Fighters. His three murderers were released under the terms of the Good Friday Agreement and one of them moved to Dundrum, County Down, the village in which Kielty was raised, and where his mother, Mary, still lives. The comedian was adamant that he harboured no sense of bitterness, and that anger never informed his act.

'It's a nice idea, isn't it, that when your father is murdered you can just put on a comedy Batman cape and start fighting evil with humour?' he told me when we met at a bar in Chelsea in the summer of 2007. 'I don't believe anger makes for great jokes. Cynicism might, to an extent, but not anger. My father was killed in a blatant sectarian attack based on the fact he was a Catholic and that he ran a business which employed people from both sides of the community. I have — with my mother and two brothers — dealt with what happened. It'd have been a lot harder if he had been implicated in terrorism in any way, but happily he wasn't.'

Kielty was preparing to follow in the footsteps of Eddie Izzard, Johnny Vegas and Billy Connolly, and try his hand as an actor in a comedy called *A Night in November* by the Olivier award-winning writer Marie Jones. He was ambitiously playing not one, but all twelve parts in the production at the old Trafalgar Studios in London. It recounted the adventures of a man from Belfast who,

Patrick Kielty with his wife, Cat Deeley.

at the time of the Shankill bombing, left his country for the first time to watch Northern Ireland play the Republic at a game of football. The only serious actor that Kielty knew then was John Standing, who, when Kielty told him what he planned to do, exclaimed, 'Darling boy, are you fucking mad?'

Kielty was nothing if not stubborn, and, having learnt his lines by playing them over and over again on his iPod, he was deemed to be up to the job after a trial run in Ireland. 'There is this mystique about acting that has been created by actors to keep people like me out. Of course I was nervous, but I took a bit of advice my father once gave me and, when I was up on stage, I just leant on the leg that was shaking the most.'

With his boyish good looks, gentle Irish brogue and quick-wittedness, Kielty had seemed born for prime-time television, and, when we met, had already had big successes hosting the BBC's *Fame Academy* and ITV's *Celebrity Love Island*. Kielty had got his picture, too, in the feelgood magazines during a long relationship with Amanda Byram, the former *Big Breakfast* presenter, and they were called 'the Posh and Becks of Northern Ireland'.

He was, however, underneath it all, always *un homme sérieux*. It's just at Queen's University in Belfast, where he studied psychology and supplemented his grant by performing a one-man comedy show, he came to see how he could communicate what he was feeling about the world as a performer. 'If you have grown up in Northern Ireland, if you have lost a parent in the Troubles, if you have grown up around people who have all lost someone, then there isn't a topic where there isn't a laugh to be had, there isn't a place that you cannot go,' he said.

Kielty knew exactly what he wanted to do with his career as a comedian, but he knew, too, that it would divide into three distinct ages. 'He starts off as the young Turk who is angry about the state of the world and wants to put it right. Then comes the age of hypocrisy — when he is still quite angry and still quite young, but quietly goes home after the show is over and puts his feet up at his nice pad in Chelsea. Then there is the final age, when he is well into middle age and making jokes about the goo-goo noises his children make. That is when he should, if he has any sense at all, give it all up.'

Patrick Kielty was born in County Down, Northern Ireland, on 31 January 1971.

Ken Dodd

One normally only gets to spend an hour or so in the company of a big star — that's the usual time limit for even the most major interviews — but, in the case of Ken Dodd, it was for three long weeks, and I don't think either of us found it especially convivial. The year was 1989, the scene, Liverpool Crown Court and the charge, tax evasion.

The celebrated comedian was then sixty-one, but already looking old and frail. George Carman, his wily QC, had told the court, doubtless to engender sympathy, that his client was suffering from 'a potentially fatal heart condition'. The case was being played out in a vast, impersonal slab of brutalist 1970s architecture, and Dodd, dressed for once in a sober suit and tie with no tickling stick in sight, looked painfully out of his comfort zone.

A number of newspapers had sent not regular court reporters to cover the case, but colour writers, such as myself, as they had imagined that Dodd playing Liverpool Crown Court would somehow be a barrel of laughs. I find it boring enough doing my own tax return, and it was hard, from the outset, to summon up much of an interest in the King of the Diddy Men's.

Brian Leveson — later ennobled and now best known for his inquiry into newspaper ethics — led for the prosecution. It was a long war of attrition that he decided to wage against Dodd which required a degree of numeracy and familiarity with accounting parlance — not to mention an appetite for tedium — that was beyond most of us.

Dodd's calling meant he had a terror of seeing anyone looking bored, and occasionally when I yawned, I'd catch his eye and he looked crestfallen. He'd joke occasionally with the journalists outside of the courtroom — 'nice day for a hanging,' he greeted us cheerily one morning — and, one afternoon, I found myself alone in a lift with him and I said I hoped he was bearing up. He shook his head sadly and said: 'I've played to better houses.'

Leveson managed to pull a few good stories out of all the bundles of documents he heaved in each day. Dodd used local children from stage schools to play the Diddy Men and had never paid them a penny. He also established that Dodd didn't trust banks. He had £336,000 in cash — equivalent to almost £1 million in today's money — stashed in suitcases in his attic. The headline writers had some fun with that — 'Doddy's Knotty Stash,' 'King of the Diddle Men' and 'the Diddled Men of Knotty Ash' all minor masterpieces — but levity was not, generally speaking, second nature to Leveson.

Dodd professed himself uneasy with money. 'I am nervous of money: nervous of having it, nervous of not having it,' he said. The case increasingly turned on whether he really understood what he was doing and was consciously being 'devious and deceitful' — as Leveson had alleged — or merely a befuddled old man with little or no idea.

For all Dodd's stage presence, the star of this particular show was unquestionably Carman, who had earlier topped the bill at the Old Bailey, where he'd managed to get the former Liberal leader, Jeremy Thorpe, acquitted on conspiracy for murder, and he'd managed, too, to get the *Coronation Street* actor Peter Adamson cleared of indecently assaulting two eight-year-old girls. In his immaculately tailored suit, Carman knew just as well as Dodd how to deliver a good line and he'd look to the jury with a sense of pride when he hit a bullseye.

'Some accountants are comedians, but comedians are never accountants,' Carman quipped at one point. I got

the impression some of his routines with Dodd had been painstakingly rehearsed. 'My grandmother was the first lady magistrate in Liverpool and also chairman of the Old Swan Labour Party,' Dodd said in the witness box. Carman: 'And she had sixteen children.' Dodd: 'She knew all about labour, yes.'

Carman could eventually add Dodd to his long list of trophy acquittals and Dodd immediately capitalised on the notoricty by playing thc London Palladium. He managed to make some jokes about what he'd been through — describing himself as 'a failed accountant' — and, his heart condition notwithstanding, he went on to live for a further twenty-nine years, dying at the age of ninety in his beloved Knotty Ash.

Ken Dodd was born in Knotty Ash, Liverpool, on 8 November, 1927, and died there on 11 March, 2018.

Sean Connery

In the age of coronavirus, it's as well perhaps not to dwell too much on six degrees of separation: the idea that all people are on average six, or fewer, social connections away from each other. Still, I was struck by how true it was when I found myself questioning Sir Sean Connery about various allegations that his former wife Diane Cilento had made about him. It was good, strong stuff with the former James Bond star telling me that Cilento was an 'insane woman' who was 'prepared to stoop to the level of the gutter' in her attempts to tarnish him.

Connery had had a son by Cilento in Jason, and, in the midst of this diatribe about his former wife, he mentioned Millfield — the school in Somerset where he had briefly sent the future *Robin of Sherwood* star — and he said it was a 'rubbish' place and that he'd bitterly regretted the decision to send him there. It so happened I had been at the school at the same time as Jason and I knew what had caused him to say this.

Jason had walked into a changing room and found a thirteen-year-old Persian boy named Mehran Sarkeshik had hanged himself. He'd tried to resuscitate him, but it was too late. Mehran had been badly bullied by an older boy. The traumatic experience caused Connery to remove Jason from the school and send him instead to Gordonstoun. Connery was still — just as much as I am — haunted by the tragedy.

Connery had a reputation for being a tough guy, and it's true he had gone on to admit that he saw nothing wrong in a husband hitting a disobedient wife, but, when I told him I'd been at Millfield at the same time as his son and had known Mehran, he spoke movingly about how, all those years on, he still felt furious about what happened. He could not understand how the school had so fundamentally failed in its duty to Mehran's parents and how he couldn't even begin to imagine the pain they must have gone through.

I'd got to know Connery through his French-Moroccan wife Micheline Roquebrune, whom I had interviewed some years before about her painting. She had always talked to me about her husband being in reality very different from his public image. 'I think it's not unhelpful for him professionally that the newspapers keep writing about what a macho guy he is, but that is not the man I know at all,' she said. 'I wouldn't have wanted to marry him if he'd been an insensitive brute. He has most certainly never hit me.'

Connery never quite came to accept that being a film star was a proper job for a grown man. His real passions had always been off-screen — Micheline, his family, golf and Scottish independence. He had long been a member of the Scottish National Party, and this, I discovered, had made for a complicated relationship with Rupert Murdoch, whose family also originated north of the border. Initially dubious about independence for Scotland, Murdoch — who is proud of his Scottish ancestry — has reportedly been coming round to the idea.

'Rupert always tells me he thinks of himself as Scottish, but you could often have fooled me,' said Connery. 'He is whatever it is expedient for him to be for tax purposes.' [1] The actor, who was making *The League of Extraordinary Gentlemen* for Murdoch's 20th Century Fox when we talked,

---

[1] During the 2014 Scottish independence referendum, Sean Connery's brother revealed that, although a lifelong supporter of the SNP, 'Sean Connery will not appear in Scotland to back the Yes campaign because of his tax exile status.'

may well have come to some kind of accommodation with him. Tellingly, when the *News of the World* was embroiled in the phone-hacking scandal, Connery let it be known that he had no interest in seeking any kind of redress from Murdoch's now-defunct tabloid.

It was in 2006 that Connery announced his retirement and resisted attempts to appear in one last Indiana Jones film for a humongous sum of money. Sir Roger Moore tried to persuade him to get together with all the other living Bond stars for one final homage to the franchise, but Connery was having none of it. He said he was finding retirement 'too much damned fun'.

Sir Sean Connery was born in Edinburgh, Scotland, on 25 August 1930, and died in the Bahamas on 31 October 2020, aged ninety.

Sean Connery with his first wife, Diane Cilento.

Roger Moore

Unfashionably, I've always considered Sir Roger Moore to be the greatest James Bond because he communicated the preposterousness of the character. Here was someone who could fly a jet plane, operate a space shuttle, a mini-submarine and ski down black runs — straight off cliffs, when, incidentally, he'd then show off his additional skills as a parachutist — and all without turning so much as a well-lacquered hair. More than that, he was a spy whose cover was so comprehensively blown that every man and his dog even knew how he liked his Martinis prepared.

That Moore played Bond for laughs encouraged the general perception he was a lightweight. I'd always assumed, too, a bit of a prima donna, so when I was delayed for more than an hour en route to interview him — a road closure following an accident — I imagined he'd have stormed off after an almighty hissy fit and there'd be an angry letter sent to my editor.

He was staying at a hotel in Cambridge, where he was appearing in a one-man show in which he reminisced about his life. Gareth Owen, his right-hand man, was waiting for me in reception. 'Well, I blew that,' I said. 'I'm sorry.' Owen told me to take a few deep breaths and led me to an all-but-deserted restaurant where, to my astonishment, Moore was still sitting with his wife Kristina Tholstrup.

They'd extended their breakfast for so long on my account that the staff were preparing the lunch settings

around them. I began apologising again. 'I gather you're doing this interview for one of Lord Rothermere's rags,' Moore said, laconically. 'So it isn't really something any of us need get terribly het up about, is it?'

Moore was then eighty-eight — he'd just over a year to live — and he joked he'd had to take his wig off as he'd got too hot. He had shed most of his hair as a result of the chemotherapy sessions he'd had to undergo for cancer. As a matter of fact, he never wore a wig on or off-screen — unlike Sir Sean Connery — and, so far from fretting about his looks, he clearly saw how absurd a thing vanity was.

My newsdesk had wanted me to ask Moore a series of fatuous questions about whether a gay man should play Bond, a handicapped man, a woman or a black man. He knew immediately what I was up to. 'Oh yes, I can see where this is going,' he said, laughing. '"Leading gay activists — take your pick here which group I should offend — reacted with fury last night to Roger Moore's suggestion that James Bond had to be played by a straight actor." Just quote me as saying I reckon the character should always be true to what Ian Fleming wrote — and you can do your worst.'

Moore was a lot smarter than he liked to let on and was a star who most certainly didn't act like a star. Indeed, he found stardom an amusing concept. He hung around a lot with Sir Michael Caine, but he marvelled at how seriously his old friend took himself. 'Michael's never got that it's all about luck. Any one of a million guys with looks and an ability to remember a few lines could have got where he is if they'd been in the right place at the right time. I get a bit tired of all this "I'm so special" stuff.'

As for his friend Sir Christopher Lee — he played the villain Scaramanga opposite Moore's Bond in *The Man With the Golden Gun* — he took a secret delight in winding him up. 'Christopher sent me a CD of him singing opera. I thanked him and said whenever I had friends round I'd play it. "Oh, Roger, I'm touched," Chris told me. And then I explained: "I like to get to bed around eleven, and, when they stay beyond that point, it's the best possible way to make them disperse."'

The interview wasn't just about Moore — he'd often defer to Kristina — and ultimately all that really mattered to either of them was that I plugged UNICEF, the children's charity for which he worked tirelessly as an ambassador. 'What honestly is the point of fame unless you put it to some worthwhile use?' he said. 'That organisation has given me the most rewarding role I ever had.'

When I heard Moore had died, I shed a few tears for a man who'd turned out to be so unexpectedly funny and forgiving. Kindness is what you remember long after you've forgotten about the stardom.

Sir Roger Moore, born in Stockwell, London, on 14 October 1927, died in Crans-Montana, Switzerland on 23 May 2017 at the age of eighty-nine.

Roger Moore with his fourth wife, Kristina Tholstrup.

Christopher Lee

There are certain parts — and Dracula is one of them — that require of the actor playing them some sense of being in on the joke with filmgoers. Sir Christopher Lee never saw anything remotely funny about what was only ever a job to him. If anything horrified him, it was a giggling stranger coming up to his wife Gitte in the street and asking if she was 'the bride of Dracula'.

He told me that insulted him every bit as much as her. He'd reminded this funster that he hadn't played the Transylvanian bloodsucker in decades. An actor can move on — and, of course, Lee did with parts in the James Bond, Star Wars and Lord of the Rings franchises — but often the fans can't, not least because, in his case, the old Hammer horrors are still a regular staple of late-night television.

Lee's friends and occasional co-stars Peter Cushing and Vincent Price took the ribbing in good part, but that wasn't Lee's way. Maybe it was because they'd both come from a traditional stage background, that they felt closer to ordinary punters. Maybe, too, Lee's wartime experiences attached to the SOE as an RAF liaison officer — when he'd often have to make decisions about whether people lived or died — had also left their mark.

Within the acting profession, Lee was often seen as stand-offish and remote. The easy-going Roger Moore couldn't help but tease him when they appeared together in *The Man With the Golden Gun.* 'He'd start off on one

of his long anecdotes on the set, and, the moment he'd turn around, Britt (Ekland) and I would run off, leaving him talking to himself,' he told me. The crew on *The Far Pavilions* struggled not to guffaw when, in the middle of a scene, Rupert Everett's horse had attempted to mount Lee's, and, in the ensuing melee, first the wig Lee was wearing for the part came off, and then his own wig, which no one was supposed to know about.

During the making of *The Three Musketeers*, Lee's co-star, Oliver Reed, had secretly spiked his orange juice with vodka. A few glasses had rendered Lee insensible. He told Reed the next day that what he had done was 'unprofessional' and refused to speak to him for some time. My guess is Reed was just trying to get him to loosen up a bit, but, when I got to know Lee around the turn of the millennium, I soon worked out that was never going to happen.

Lee was more often than not oblivious to how other people saw him. He told me, with genuine incredulity, how, when he'd been walking along a street close to his home, he'd spotted Dirk Bogarde, with whom he'd appeared in *A Tale of Two Cities* in 1958, and said a cheery 'hello'. Bogarde, not even breaking his stride, had said simply: 'Yes, Christopher, I know, but it was all a very long time ago.'

Still, it was probably Lee's sense of utter conviction in his all-too-often preposterous films that had made him a hero of mine as I was growing up. 'Every actor has to make terrible movies from time to time,' he said, 'but the trick is not to be terrible in them.' After I'd done my first interview with him — when he'd joked I seemed to remember a lot more about his career than he did — he was happy to meet for a series of lunches at Le Caprice and his club, Buck's. He was then in his eighties, but his work — or, more to the point, his income stream — mattered to him as much as ever.

It meant he could be ruthless. Cushing was an infinitely bigger star than Lee when Hammer Films first teamed them up in 1957 in *The Curse of Frankenstein,* but, towards the end of the following decade, Lee told his agent to write it into his contract that his name should come before Cushing's in opening credits. 'It was just that I was by then the more bankable name,' Lee said, matter-of-factly, when I'd inquired. 'Peter never said anything about it, but his wife Helen told me it was hurtful.'

Occasionally, Lee would admit to disappointments — if only he'd got the part of the old butler in *The Remains of the Day* and he regretted turning down the role Leslie Nielsen ended up making his own in the *Airplane!* films — but, mostly, he had run his career with an almost infallible business acumen. In the 1970s, as Cushing kept churning out increasingly ropey films for Hammer out of a sense of loyalty, Lee saw there was no use staying on in Britain, where the industry was starting to go into sharp decline, and decamped to Los Angeles. It was a typically canny move, and a part in *Airport '77* turned out to be the first in a remunerative series of blockbusters.

Lee eventually came back to Britain — residing in some style in a vast apartment near Sloane Square in London — and a knighthood ensued. His fellow actors might not have been so sure he deserved it — Dame Eileen Atkins felt such honours ought to be the preserve of theatre luminaries — but Lee got to have the last laugh. He was still working when he died in 2015 at the age of ninety-three and had probably made more money than any actor of his generation.

Sir Christopher Lee, born in Belgravia, London, on 27 May 1922, died in Chelsea, London, on 7 June 2015, at the age of ninety-three.

Peter Vaughan

What Shakespeare called the Seventh Age of Man was turning out to be a money-spinner for Peter Vaughan. The actor — best known perhaps as Grouty in the television series *Porridge* — was eighty-four when we met and enthusiastically promoting a film directed by Frank Oz called *Death at a Funeral*. It was, in all honesty, hardly his greatest work, but it was work and work is what has always mattered in the acting profession.

I'd lunched with Vaughan's fellow octogenarian Sir Christopher Lee not long before and he confided in me how irked he had been not to have bagged the part of Mr Stevens Snr, the father of Sir Anthony Hopkins' repressed butler in *The Remains of the Day*. 'There are unfortunately a lot of us old guys around,' Vaughan said. 'These roles are always scene-stealers and they can define entire careers, so the stakes are high. Actors vying for them are conscious, too, that their time is running out so it's often a bare-knuckle fight.'

It's not hard to see why the director James Ivory cast Vaughan as that old-school professional, determined to ensure that 'everything is in hand'. He was not unlike the actor. There was a scene in the film in which a droplet of water fell from his nose into a bowl of soup that he was serving. Vaughan thought nothing of having a painful solution put up his nostril that caused the required droplet to fall precisely on cue. He didn't even think to ask if it would do him any harm.

Peter Vaughan with Ronnie Barker in the BBC's *Porridge*.

Even in comedies, such as the film he was promoting, Vaughan approached the work with deadly seriousness. 'When I was making *Straw Dogs*, the director Sam Peckinpah got all the actors together and told us he never wanted to see us laughing at each other again, because, when actors are conscious that they are funny, they cease to be funny,' he said. 'He was absolutely right, of course.' He said that he and his wife Lillias had been 'appalled' to see a play, the night before I interviewed him, in which the actors had broken out into uncontrollable laughter on stage. 'It was,' he said coldly, 'unprofessional and theatre tickets don't come cheap.'

Vaughan's big break had been playing the homosexual character, Ed, in Joe Orton's *Entertaining Mr Sloane* at Wyndham's Theatre in 1964. It was a brave part at that time, but Vaughan could see the impact it would have. He also liked Orton. 'Joe was a one-off. He would always wear army boots, a Chairman Mao jacket and an old War Department gas mask bag over his shoulder in which he had his meat pie for lunch and his copy of the script. If I asked him about a line, he'd tell me it means whatever I want it to mean. He respected actors. Harold Pinter would say the same thing, and, years later, when I was making the film *The Crucible*, so did Arthur Miller.'

One critic noted that Vaughan could convey menace reading a weather report. He accepts his 'bloody awful war' was probably a factor in how he came across. He served in Normandy and Belgium, as an officer, which he said was 'terrifying'. Later, in the Far East, he was at the liberation of Changi jail. 'It was a strange way, between the ages of eighteen and twenty-four, to form a character,' he said. 'I think I was in a daze when I came back to Britain, after seeing what I saw. It took me a while to come to terms with it.'

His first marriage, to the actress Billie Whitelaw, didn't last, he reckoned, as he hadn't been good at communicating emotions. He'd learnt to be 'a lot more human' when he married, not long after he parted from Whitelaw in 1966, Lillias Walker, also an actress. That union lasted until his death. He was working until the very end — his final role was as Maester Aemon in *Game of Thrones* — and I well remember him scoffing when I mentioned the word 'retirement'. 'This is no time to take it easy — I am in my prime,' he said, quite seriously.

Peter Vaughan, born in Wem, Shropshire, on 4 April 1923, died in Mannings Heath, West Sussex, on 6 December 2016 at the age of ninety-three.

Donald Sinden

I first met Donald Sinden in the mid-1980s when I showed up too early at his home in Golders Green in north London. He came to the door in his dressing gown and slippers and with his hair all over the place and told me he wasn't quite ready. It was nearly midday, but actors keep different hours from the rest of us, and so I took a walk around the block and came back at the appointed time.

Sinden had in the meantime got on his public face, which meant he was booted, suited and brilliantined. It was an old-fashioned look, even then, and there was something about his whole demeanour that seemed to invite ridicule. The satirical puppet show *Spitting Image* was at the time portraying him as an incurable old ham, who was desperate for a knighthood. Regional accents, five o'clock shadow and naturalism had become the norm for actors since the kitchen sink dramas of the 1960s, but Sinden was having none of it. He was still defiantly making a point of not only looking like he had just walked off the set of one of his old Rank films, like *Doctor in the House,* but also enunciating every syllable perfectly and poshly.

He looked at me uncomprehendingly when I broached these subjects. He insisted he'd never thought for a moment about a knighthood, and, as for the new style of acting, he happened to feel 'drawing rooms are eminently more comfortable to sit in than kitchen sinks'. He had been trained at the Webber Douglas Academy of Dramatic

Art, and he was damned if, as a secondary schoolboy from a humble home in Plymouth, he was going to unlearn what they'd taught him.

Sinden's failure to move with the times could sometimes, of course, be embarrassing. In 1979, he was one of the last actors to be willing to 'black up' to play *Othello,* but he told me he could see nothing wrong about it because Laurence Olivier had done the very same thing. He couldn't see that society had moved on since 1964.

He could also be a professional snob: he wasn't remotely impressed, for instance, with Clark Gable, who starred with him in the Hollywood adventure film *Mogambo.* He described him as 'a lorry driver who'd got it into his head he could act'. He added that, while filming on location in equatorial Africa, he'd had the misfortune to have a tent

Donald Sinden with Peggy Cummins in
Your Money or Your Wife (1959).

MARC SINDEN
MS PRODUCTIONS
for
THE ONE NIGHT
BOOKING COMPANY
presents

AN
EVENING
WITH...

Sir
Donald Sinden

beside Gable's and was kept awake most nights as he set about bedding virtually the entire female cast. 'The noise made my stomach churn,' said Sinden.

If I lampooned Sinden in the piece I wrote back then, he was lampooning himself every bit as much in television sitcoms, such as *Two's Company* and *Never the Twain.*

In the former, he was sent up by an irreverent American writer played by Elaine Stritch, and, in the latter, Windsor Davies' rough-and-ready antique dealer.

The fates decreed that was not to be my last encounter with Sinden, and, in the ensuing decades, I found myself interviewing him or meeting him socially again and again. Whether he had actually forgotten or chose to forget my first piece, I will never know, but his good humour and remorseless cheerfulness eventually began to wear me down.

He finally got his knighthood in 1997 and his profession came, also, to appreciate him. I well remember the warmth in the applause he received for his last stage performance as an ageing opera star in a revival of Ronald Harwood's play *Quartet* in 1999.

Ultimately, Sinden couldn't help being himself. When, in 2014, I telephoned him for a comment about the death of Elaine Stritch, his first reaction was 'rejoice, rejoice'. Stritch had made his life hell during the filming of *Two's Company.* He was doubling up in a West End stage production in the evenings and found the endless retakes necessitated by her heavy drinking physically exhausting. After explaining all of that, he remembered his public persona and said that, on second thoughts, could I please just quote him as saying he was 'very sad that Miss Stritch had died'.

The last time I saw Sinden, it was in a restaurant when, not long before his death, he did a spot of table-hopping, and, for a few happy moments, he joined mine. He cracked a series of jokes and I remember looking at him and wondering why I'd expended so much time trying to analyse such an uncomplicated man. Even when he was almost ninety, he never lost that childlike need to please and to make people happy.

Sir Donald Sinden was born in Plymouth, Devon, on 9 October 1923, and died in Wittersham, Kent, on 12 September 2014, at the age of ninety.

Julio Iglesias

I got to meet the old crooner Julio Iglesias in the late 1980s and saw a side to him that's generally kept well hidden from the public.

In those days, I used to work with Jane Bown, a photographer so grand that she numbered the Queen among her personal friends. It was the talk of *The Observer* office that she'd once stayed at Balmoral with her husband Martin Moss, who ran Simpsons of Piccadilly. Her Majesty commissioned her to take one of her official birthday portraits.

Jane needed to be handled every bit as carefully as the trickiest of interviewees: she always insisted on working with natural light and so her principal anxiety was the sun going down. She hated it when people smiled — 'a smile gets annoying if you look at a photograph for a long time' — and she placed all the emphasis on the eyes of her subjects. She certainly didn't care about offending anybody and once interrupted an intense interview I was doing with Prince Paul of Romania to tell me in a stage whisper: 'It's his face. It's all wrong and I just can't make it work.'

And so it was, nerve-rackingly late one winter afternoon, we arrived at the Dorchester to meet Julio, the Spanish singer, songwriter and former professional footballer. In the taxi, Jane had been adamant that she would do what she called her 'snaps' first as time was getting on and I was to keep out of it.

The moment we were ushered into Julio's presence, she whipped out her little Olympus OM-1 and started clicking. He put his hands up to shield himself. 'On no account,' he decreed, 'are there to be any photographs of the left side of my face. She is taking photographs of my left side. There, she has just done it again. I will not do this interview unless you give me a firm undertaking.'

He addressed himself to me as if I was somehow directing operations. This was his misapprehension. Jane looked out of the window of his suite at the sun going down, then at him and finally at me in despair. A long, awkward silence ensued between the three of us.

I moved in to try to diffuse the diplomatic stand-off. I examined first the left side of Julio's face and then the right. I could in all honesty see very little difference between the two vistas, but for the fact his hairline had retreated a little on the left, where he had parted it. Still, I nodded solemnly, said I saw what Julio was getting at and asked Jane if she would mind awfully taking her pictures from his right side.

She snorted in derision. 'I never had this problem with Margaret Thatcher, whose picture I took only last week,' she said. 'You're weak, Tim. Weak, weak, weak. And as for this man...'

I retorted that I didn't see it as an issue that was fundamental to the freedom of the press and added that I really would at some point like to ask my questions. Julio was a witness to our little contretemps and it was his turn to try to be peacemaker. 'Look, you two, there's no use falling out over this,' he said. 'I do know what is best. The left side of my face, well, it isn't any good. It isn't what your readers would want to see. We really all have to play the game.'

Jane moved with poor grace to his right-hand side, grumbled that, on top of it all, he kept smiling, and, between weary sighs, started clicking intermittently, but her heart was clearly no longer in it.

A rare picture of the left side of Julio Iglesias.

Julio then started going on at some length about his teeth. 'Every time I go up in an aeroplane, it leaves me with toothache,' he said, pointing at his dazzlingly white pearlies. 'I've talked to some of the most eminent dentists in the world and there is nothing they can do.'

I was mindful we were thirty minutes into a forty-minute slot with Julio and I had still to ask a single question. There's normally time to build up to a difficult subject, but I had to go for broke. I wondered if, as he was emerging from the wrong side of middle age, he envisaged a problem sustaining his image as a great romantic.

'You've waited this long and that's all you can think of to ask me?' He said. 'Oh well, very well. Obviously, I have these looks that make people think I am this great Don Juan, but, I mean, if you believed all the stories that have been written about me — that I have taken 3,000 women to bed, for instance — well, I would have died of exhaustion by now, or something a lot worse.'

I dutifully scribbled it down, allowed him to talk for a few moments about the concert he was about to do in London and then his PR woman came in to tell us our allotted time was up. I protested as she ushered us out that I'd only got to ask one question.

Jane and I shared a taxi back to the office in stony silence. When the interview was published, I was unstartled to see it was accompanied by an enormous photograph of Julio that showed the world, in all its glory, his left side.

Julio Iglesias was born in Madrid in Spain on 23 September 1943.

'Every time I go up in an aeroplane, it leaves me with toothache,' said Iglesias.

Harry Andrews

When I arrived at the home of Harry Andrews in the Sussex countryside, I was greeted at the door by his lover of the past thirty years, who led me into the living room where the 'tough guy' star of war films such as *The Hill, The Red Beret* and *Battle of Britain* was waiting with a pot of tea, a plate of biscuits and a broad, gap-toothed smile.

Andrews was one of those actors who possessed a face that was disproportionately more famous than his name. Years of appearing on the boards with Olivier, Gielgud and Richardson meant, however, that his status within his profession was assured.

This was the mid-1980s and Andrews had just landed a part in *Dynasty*, the hit television series that starred Joan Collins and John Forsythe. He was apprehensive. 'They told me how many people tuned in to watch,' he said. 'It depresses me to think that more people will see me in just one episode of this than all of my stage work put together.'

He didn't like the idea, either, that it might turn him into a 'celebrity'. Andrews loathed the word, very rarely gave interviews, and had, in his younger days, turned down the chance of a Hollywood contract, supposedly because he'd baulked at having to pin back his much-too-big ears and change his much-too-forgettable name. This was an actor who had clearly made a conscious decision to be no more famous than absolutely necessary.

A factor in this may well have been the lover who had opened the door to me: Basil Hoskins, a popular character actor who had appeared in television series such as *Emergency Ward 10*, *The Prisoner* and also, with Andrews, the classic war film *Ice Cold in Alex*. Andrews' private life was no secret among his peers — the Oliviers would entertain him and Hoskins at their home in nearby Steyning — but he had never made any kind of public announcement about it, and no wonder because homosexuality had, for most of his career, been a criminal offence. The most Andrews had ever done was to hint at it in later life when he had accepted the part of an overtly gay character in the film version of Joe Orton's *Entertaining Mr Sloane*.

Andrews was great fun to talk to and he could not have been more easy-going, but professionalism was obviously what mattered to him more than anything. He spoke of his disgust that Marlon Brando, when he had appeared with him in a scene in *Superman*, insisted that 'idiot boards', with his lines written on them, were placed behind the cameras. 'They were paying him millions of dollars for just a few days' work and it's not like he had that many lines to learn,' he said. 'I looked at Trevor (Howard) who was in the scene, too, and we both raised our eyes to the heavens.'

He felt Richard Burton, after marrying Elizabeth Taylor, had allowed his celebrity to get in the way of his acting, which he had a duty to put first. He admitted he had no time for actors who failed to appear on sets or stages on time: he expected them to be word-perfect, sober and ready to start.

In contrast to the characters he played on screen, Andrews detested war. 'I saw close friends blown to bits beside me,' he said. 'No one who has been through that could find war glamorous.' Still, he made it into the Queen's Royal Kent Regiment, took part in the D-Day landings and

Harry Andrews often played tough military roles.

was mentioned in despatches. He was also — 'briefly', he pointed out — promoted to the rank of major.

Peaceful pursuits, such as gardening, music and reading occupied the real Andrews' time, and, as for the roles coming his way, he cheerfully conceded he'd cornered the market in 'deathbed scenes'. He'd died in the television series *Clayhanger*, confided he was expected to slip the mortal coil, too, in *Dynasty*, and had most recently conked out in a show called *Inside Story*, in which he played a newspaper proprietor. He had several scenes with the former Prime Minister Harold Wilson in a cameo role. 'I got on very well with his wife, but Wilson himself was very boring. All his conversations with me started: "Of course, when I was prime minister..."'

I hadn't the slightest idea about Andrews' sexuality until I'd arrived at his home — not a word even hinting at it had appeared up until then in the newspapers — but, at seventy-three, he obviously couldn't be bothered to pretend any more. This posed a moral dilemma for me as an ambitious, young, local newspaper journalist: if I got into the issue at all in the interview, I knew there was a grim inevitability about what would ensue. The homophobia of the tabloids was virulent in those days because of AIDS, and the coverage of the last days of Rock Hudson — another *Dynasty* star — had been peculiarly tasteless and judgemental. Did I really want it on my conscience I had put not just Andrews, but also Hoskins, through a lot of lurid 'gay secret' headlines in their later years?

This was a scoop I decided I could do without, and, after my interview appeared — focusing on Andrews' career — I received a handwritten note from him in which he'd described me as a 'civilised interrogator'. He passed away peacefully four years later and was able to 'come out' on his own terms, and posthumously. In 2005, when Hoskins also died, he was, as Andrews had asked, buried beside him in the graveyard at St Mary the Virgin in Salehurst, East Sussex.

Harry Andrews was born in Tonbridge, Kent, on 10 November 1911, and died in Salehurst, Sussex, on 6 March 1989, at the age of seventy-seven.

Quentin Crisp

Quentin Crisp was fond of saying that if you ever wanted to shock your parents, you should tell them you'd spent some time in his company. I'm not sure if he was all that shocking by the time I caught up with him, in 1985, when he was about to do a one-man show at the Theatre Royal in Brighton. *The Naked Civil Servant*, the television drama based on his early life, had come out a decade before and had turned him into something of a national treasure. He preferred to call himself 'one of the country's great stately homos', even if, by that point, he was living in a famously messy apartment in New York.

Sure, his hair was dyed blue, he wore rouge and mascara and he talked and walked like Lady Bracknell, but he seemed a cosy and unthreatening adornment, adding nothing but gaiety to nations. And, oh yes, he was without question an actor. He told me his whole life had really been an act. Even as a boy, his mother could see that he'd make a perfect fairy in a school production of *A Midsummer Night's Dream*. She permitted him to wear her green tulle and garlands for the occasion.

In his later years, he built up a respectable body of work on stage and on film, sometimes playing himself in cameos, notably in the Oscar-winning *Philadelphia*, but also in proper roles such as Dr Zalhus in the trendy Sting horror film *The Bride*, and, in an inspired piece of casting, Queen Elizabeth I in *Orlando,* alongside Tilda Swinton and Billy Zane.

We'd met for tea at the Grand Hotel and he was dressed in a mauve trouser suit with matching fedora. I suppose when somebody looks very striking, there is always an expectation that they will say striking things. I found Crisp rather disappointing in that regard. He spoke for a very long time about how the weather was playing havoc with his lumbago.

I'd also got it into my head that he was a brave warrior in the fight for LGBT rights, and, while he was undoubtedly courageous in his early life, he'd latterly started to bat for the other side. 'I see gay men as observers, by which I mean they don't really participate in life in the way that others do. I mean they don't have wives and children and responsibilities and so it's not quite the same for them. They are not fully invested in society.'

Taken aback, I asked him if he even supported the gay rights movement, and he wondered if such 'a diverse and incongruous group of people' could really be called a movement at all. He said he wasn't clear about what it was 'they' wanted to achieve. I was writing the piece for the *Evening Argus* in Brighton, a city which had, of course, a big homosexual community, and it was difficult to know where to even begin without causing enormous offence.

It seemed to me there was more than enough homophobia at the time — this was at the height of the AIDS epidemic — without one of the country's best-known homosexuals compounding it. I quoted him judiciously. In later interviews, Crisp went on to say still more incendiary things about homosexuality, which right-wing newspapers happily lapped up. He described homosexuality as 'a terrible disease' and said 'the world would be better without homosexuals'. He told *The Times* that he would advise parents to abort a foetus if it could be shown to be genetically predetermined to be gay.

The gay rights campaigner Peter Tatchell wondered if Crisp was really just outraged that he was no longer

Quentin Crisp played Queen Elizabeth I in the film *Orlando* (1992).

the centre of attention. Perhaps he disliked being overshadowed by other gays. As Tatchell memorably observed, they'd 'queered his pitch.'

Still, unlike Larry Grayson and John Inman, Crisp never really fell out of fashion. This may well be precisely because he fitted in with a certain kind of outdated notion of what a homosexual should be, which is to say apologetic. For myself, I found Crisp charmless, tedious and ultimately mystifying. I think he loved playing to the crowd, but hadn't really worked out what to say to it or at least to come up with a narrative that was consistent.

When I got back to the office, a colleague mentioned he'd spotted us at the Grand. 'Who on earth was that you were with?' he asked. I'd mischievously replied: 'Oh, just my dad.'

Quentin Crisp was born in Sutton in Surrey on 25 December 1908, and died in Manchester on 21 November 1999, aged ninety.

Quentin Crisp, in his famously squalid New York apartment, photographed by Graham MacIndoe in 1993.

Rupert Everett

Rupert Everett was nudging fifty when I met him at a restaurant in Soho. He was promoting the paperback edition of his autobiography *Red Carpets and Other Banana Skins*. Anyone who has read the book, with its wittily acerbic portrait of Hollywood, could reasonably have expected its author to be a thrilling cross between Noël Coward and Gore Vidal. Those expectations he dashed soon enough.

He talked a lot about the disappointments and frustrations of his career, and I asked him, after a while, if he felt a greater degree of fame was due to him. 'I think being famous has become rather common, actually,' he replied, lugubriously. 'I don't really respect the sort of people who get to be famous. That whole world doesn't seem at all glamorous any more — the films aren't glamorous, the music isn't and the people you see getting out of the private jets aren't. I think there is something rather tragic about it all, actually.'

On the stock market of show business, Everett's valuation was once well in excess of Colin Firth — with whom he appeared, at the age of twenty-two, in *Another Country,* and, more recently, *The Happy Prince* — but, as we spoke in the summer of 2007, it had, after some wild fluctuations, settled at a point some way beneath his old friend and rival.

Everett felt it could be blamed to a large extent on the fact he was gay. Nigel Dempster, the *Daily Mail* gossip columnist, was the first to start hinting about it in the

eighties, but Everett didn't actually 'come out' until January 1995 in an interview with the *Daily Express*, and then, three months later, after no one appeared to notice, he came out again to the *Mail*. And then he told a journalist from the *Independent* that he had, as a struggling young actor, briefly supplemented his income from prostitution, and, again, the nation appeared unstartled. Then he repeated it to an American journalist and suddenly all hell broke loose.

'The difference was I had made *My Best Friend's Wedding* in the meantime and the second time that story was published it was in America,' he explained. 'I hadn't anticipated that nation's puritanism. I think there is an expectation that all those of us who live under the American empire should conform. It is very difficult to be who you are. We are all as a consequence becoming very Tony Blairy.'

Everett didn't believe cinema-goers could generally care less what stars did in the privacy of their own bedrooms, but he felt it obsessed risk-averse studio executives. 'I think they are very prejudiced. I am allowed to play Prince Charming in *Shrek* because it is a cartoon, but I would never be allowed to take such a heterosexual part in a film and certainly not James Bond.'

Once everybody knew he was gay, he chose not to be a particularly enthusiastic champion for the gay community. He admitted to taking a rather 'old-fashioned' line on some gay issues, such as adoption. 'Oh, God, I could never do that to a child. Can you imagine what it would be like having your two dads coming to school speech days? And hearing those awful queeny rows while you are trying to get to sleep?' Of many of the rights now enjoyed by gays, he was ambivalent. 'I think that young gay guys are imprisoned by their very freedoms, funnily enough. They are imprisoned by looks and categories. They certainly seem to me no freer than the homosexuals who were once illegal.'

It was a downbeat and self-indulgent lunch and I found it hard to reconcile the Everett I met in the flesh with the Everett I had met in the book, and, indeed, on screen and on stage. On form, Everett can be sensational. I first saw him on stage in Coward's *The Vortex* in 1989 and he made the production smoulder with passion. Later, in what was originally intended to be a minor role in *My Best Friend's Wedding*, he ended up outclassing Julia Roberts and making the film his own. He communicated a hilarious world-weariness as the debauched Prince of Wales in *The Madness of King George*, and, more recently, in *The Happy Prince*, he was profoundly moving as the dying Oscar Wilde.

Everett was aware that my job involved reviewing theatre and asked if he could periodically be my plus-one. We went to a number of shows together — raising a few eyebrows among my fellow critics — and there were some lunches and dinners, but the conversations almost invariably revolved around him and his frustrations. I realised, after a while, that I wanted to like Everett a lot more than I actually did.

Rupert Everett was born on 29 May 1959.

John Schlesinger

John Schlesinger resided in one of those vast Christmas cake mansions in Kensington that signal to all the world its owner has achieved his wildest dreams. He couldn't exactly claim to be a self-made man — Dad had been a wealthy physician and Mum a stockbroker's daughter — but he'd made his name and his own fortune in the perilously insecure world of theatre and later film directing.

The year was 1991 and he was promoting *Pacific Heights*, a film he had directed that starred Michael Keaton and Melanie Griffith. A guy was leaving as I was arriving and Schlesinger, oblivious to me, gave him a peck on the lips. He had been 'out' as a gay man long before homosexual acts had been legalised. He hadn't felt the need to get married — as his friend and fellow director Tony Richardson had — or to show up at premières with a woman on his arm. His daring, groundbreaking film *Sunday Bloody Sunday* — its gay protagonist played by Peter Finch had lived in a square just around the corner — he had called a 'personal statement'.

He had the kettle boiled and he made me a cup of acrid herbal tea. These sort of interviews are normally conducted in hotel suites, but it was typical of Schlesinger that he should do it at his home as he was a man who couldn't be bothered to hide anything at all about himself. We talked only briefly about *Pacific Heights*. He said he knew very well it wasn't his best film, but it was a taut, efficient

psychological thriller that, as he said, 'did what it said on the tin.'

Schlesinger was a big man with a big personality and he seemed to see the world from a higher plain. He had a way of cutting through all the nonsense in his work and his life. He also rather enjoyed shocking. Of *Midnight Cowboy* — his 1969 film about a male street hustler — he said he asked himself how far he should go with it and he went pretty much all the way. It became the first and only X-rated film to win Best Picture in the Academy Awards, in addition to Best Adapted Screenplay and Best Director.

He laughed when I asked him why he'd put his name to an open letter defending the actor and gay rights activist Ian McKellen's decision to accept a knighthood from John Major's 'family values' government. 'I could hear a particular sound in my head the morning it was published. It was the teacups clinking disdainfully on to saucers in Cheltenham as little old ladies said to each other, "My dear, it's so unnecessary." But I'm afraid I just didn't care as it seemed to me it was the right thing to do.'

At the National Theatre, during all the behind-the-scenes politicking in the 1970s, he had been enormously supportive to his fellow director Michael Blakemore when he'd dared to challenge its boss, Sir Peter Hall, about all the money he was making from his outside ventures. Later he had sensed, too, the vulnerability of the National's ousted artistic director, Laurence Olivier, and put in a call to offer him the unlikely part of a Nazi dentist in the thriller *Marathon Man*. It set the great actor off on a new career path and led to him calling Schlesinger nothing less than the 'restorer' of his life.

It was typical of Schlesinger that he insisted Olivier's character should be seen to scrupulously wash his hands

John Schlesinger directs Jon Voight and Dustin Hoffman in *Midnight Cowboy* (1969).

before setting about torturing Dustin Hoffman in his dentist's chair. 'It's because that's what a real dentist would have instinctively done,' Schlesinger said. 'Humanity with all of its absurd ironies has always fascinated me. I want people, when they watch my films, to see underneath the fingernails of the characters. I want them to see all the dirt. I don't believe in characters in films who don't have any imperfections. I don't believe, for example, in Rocky.'

My own favourite Schlesinger film had been *An Englishman Abroad*, which he'd made for the BBC. It recounted how the actress Coral Browne had befriended the spy Guy Burgess while appearing in a play in Moscow. Browne had played herself in the drama and made a big success of it. She was a friend of Schlesinger and he was desperately worried about her as she was, when we'd met, entering what turned out to be the final stages of her battle with cancer. 'I've reached the point in my life when so many of the people I love are dying,' he said. 'Makes me more aware than ever that we might as well say what we really feel.'

Schlesinger died thirteen years later, at seventy-seven, survived by his partner of over thirty years, the photographer Michael Childers.

John Schlesinger was born in Hampstead, London, on 16 February 1926, and died on 25 July 2003, in Palm Spings, California.

Richard Chamberlain

In the 1970s, my family were close to the owners of the Bear Hotel at Woodstock. Kenneth More knew them, too, and was there a lot during the making of the film *The Slipper and the Rose*, as Broughton Castle, not far away in Banbury, was used as a location. Richard Chamberlain was the star and a lot of girls would come up to More and ask if he could introduce them. He'd chuckle and always reply that they'd better not get their hopes up as 'women aren't really his thing'. It became something of a running joke.

Years later, I was tasked with interviewing Chamberlain when he was making a television film in London called *The Bourne Identity*. I was reminded of what More had said as I leafed through the newspaper cuttings. What had at first seemed unthinkable — when he was the all-American embodiment of heterosexuality in a series of romantic leads — had started to be hinted at and then spelt out more obviously and cruelly. This was 1988 when the AIDS epidemic was at its height and just about all the tabloid newspapers were homophobic.

The day of our interview there was a story in one of them about how Chamberlain had not gone to the funeral of a man who'd died of AIDS. The piece implied he had been a lover of Chamberlain, and, if this was true, I could well understand why, at that time, he'd decided to keep away.

We'd met over two servings of fish and chips in the canteen at Twickenham Studios in south-west London. His white shirt was covered in 'Kensington Gore' — fake blood — after he'd just done a fight scene and I joked

Richard Chamberlain in *The Slipper and the Rose* (1976).

about how it looked like he'd had a terrible accident with the ketchup. Chamberlain didn't laugh. He was then in his early fifties, still strikingly handsome and with all the grandeur about him that comes with long-term Hollywood stardom.

It was clear, however, that he didn't enjoy press interviews. The story in the tabloid had understandably set him on edge. His PR man was adamant that there were to be no questions about his private life. 'I enjoy the acting,' Chamberlain said, 'but not the fame. It's a pity you can't have one without the other.' He recognised that he 'owed' *Dr Kildare* for helping to make his name, but he said if he'd ever met the character he could have gladly decked him. 'I used to argue with the scriptwriters and ask why he had to be so exasperatingly perfect all the time. It made it boring for me as an actor and it created a whole generation of fans who had an idea of me that bore absolutely no relation to the truth.'

Chamberlain had since managed to play the occasional baddie — he'd had a lot of fun as the purveyor of dodgy electrical cables in *The Towering Inferno* — but he understood the importance of preserving an image. When a photographer from my paper showed up, he spent several minutes contorting his facial muscles, which made for a comical spectacle. The photographer explained to me afterwards he'd seen a lot of American actors doing it — Stirling Hayden, among them — and the fanciful idea was that they could temporarily iron out the lines on their faces before a picture was taken.

As I was leaving I said to Chamberlain that it made it difficult for me to write a rounded story with no reference to his private life. 'A lot of pieces have been written about me that have caused me pain,' he said.

At the age of sixty-eight, Chamberlain finally informed an unstartled world that he was gay.

Richard Chamberlain was born in Beverly Hills, California, on 31 March 1934.

Antony Sher

Sir Antony Sher was presented to the Queen at the Prince of Wales's fiftieth birthday party at Buckingham Palace. 'He is one of our leading actors, ma'am,' explained Sir Geoffrey Cass, who was then the chairman of the Royal Shakespeare Company, to Her Majesty. She frowned, paused for a very long time and finally said, 'Oh, *are* you?'

A riposte, mercifully unuttered, formed in Sher's head. 'No, of course not, Your Majesty, you've seen through me. I'm just a little gay Yid from somewhere called Sea Point on the other side of the world. I shouldn't be here. I don't know why I am. I'm an impostor.' That was how Sher was at the time — an angry, if not incandescent, outsider — but psychotherapy, a civil partnership, a knighthood, and, funnily enough, a convivial enough stay at Sandringham as a house guest of the heir to the throne, all seemed to have mellowed him.

It was the summer of 2007, and we were chatting in his dressing room at the Apollo Theatre in London, where he was preparing to open in the title role of *Kean*. 'All the anger that I've had has actually worked out rather well for me,' he said. 'Certainly, I wouldn't have had the career I've had without it.'

It had been two years since Sher had last appeared on stage in *Primo* on Broadway. He had wanted time out to focus on his painting and writing. He had also wanted to see if he could survive without acting, which, clearly, he could not. His comeback role, playing Edmund Kean,

Antony Sher in *Hysteria* (1993).

was, he said, too good to resist. The legendary nineteenth century actor was something of an inspiration to him.

When, in 1968, he had come to Britain from his native South Africa, the most celebrated actors were Olivier, Gielgud and Richardson. All were tall, well-spoken and conventionally handsome. Sher was Jewish, diminutive and had a pronounced South African accent. 'Kean gave me great heart because he broke the mould — he was illegitimate, born into semi-poverty, and he, too, was short and dark and his voice was not usual. This was someone who defied the rules, and, of course, he had, too, his demons.'

There was another similarity: addiction. Kean had sought salvation in alcohol and Sher in cocaine. Sher was once in the closet about all three of his most defining characteristics — not merely his homosexuality, but also his nationality and his faith. He had last visited a synagogue when he was thirteen. He had tried getting married to a woman — a fact that goes unrecorded in his *Who's Who* entry — and, when giving interviews to newspapers, there was a time when he would ask his publicists to tell journalists to keep off his private life. 'It was, of course, like putting a gigantic neon sign over my head, saying "This guy is gay",' he wryly observed.

When, in 1989, he finally came out, he said the announcement precipitated what he called 'an outbreak of gayness' in the Sher family. 'My elder sister came out, too, after twenty-five years of marriage, and one of my nieces, as well. It was clearly catching.' His mother had felt it would probably be best not to tell his father, but, when he found out, Sher said that his reaction had been unexpectedly loving and it had the effect of bringing them closer.

He used to say that the happiest day of his life had been in 1979 when he was granted a British passport and burnt his South African one. That day, he said, had since been surpassed. That was when, on 21 December 2005, he entered into a civil partnership with Gregory Doran, at the time an associate director of the Royal Shakespeare Company. 'There are hard-line gay activists who say that it isn't good enough. It's not called a marriage. I don't care. I can call Greg my next of kin and that is what matters.'

Sir Antony Sher was born in Cape Town, South Africa, on 14 June 1949.

Michael Winner

The late *Daily Mail* gossip columnist Nigel Dempster loved to have a flutter. When I worked as his deputy around the turn of the millennium, he'd be watching the racing on television most afternoons. On one occasion, Michael Winner, the director best known for the *Death Wish* films, was being randomly interviewed at some race meeting and was holding forth on the runners and riders. He was wearing a vast puffer jacket with multiple zips and pockets. Dempster, cackling, reached for his phone and called Winner's mobile.

We saw Winner panicking as his *Copacabana* ringtone sounded, desperately trying to find the pocket in which he'd placed his mobile, and, just when it looked like he was about to locate it, Dempster hung up. Then, when Winner started talking again, Dempster called once more, and again the *Copacabana* drowned him out. This ritual was repeated over and over. It was a form of interactive television that had the whole diary office crying with laughter.

When, in September 2003, it was announced Dempster was retiring on account of ill health, I was working for *The Sunday Telegraph* and wrote a piece paying tribute to the old boy and recalled the Winner story. When it was published, Winner telephoned my editor and disputed it had ever happened and an angry letter from him, that effectively accused me of lying, appeared in the newspaper the following week.

Channel 4 Racing told me they hadn't the resources to unearth the clip and Dempster himself was at that point

unfortunately too ill to express a view one way or the other. Happily, Meryl La Trobe, who had been Dempster's personal assistant, had seen Winner's letter. She wrote in to confirm that she recalled the incident every bit as vividly as I did, and her letter, the following week, was also published.

I'd formed the impression a long time ago that Winner was a nasty piece of work. Margaret Levin, an old friend who presided over Wiltons restaurant in St James's, had warned me he was 'vile'. He'd savaged her in a restaurant review he had written for *The Sunday Times* because she refused to be bullied by him. Neil Libbert, an affable *Observer* photographer I knew, had meanwhile told me how he'd once tried to park outside Winner's home in Holland Park. 'Out he came and stood in the place and told me to "fuck off",' Libbert told me. 'I said, "This is a public street, I'm entitled to park here," and he said "no you're not, fuck off, it's the law of the fucking jungle here".'

Before our very public row, Winner had asked me out for lunch several times, but I'd always declined as he struck me as a preposterous figure. He hadn't made a film in years and all he had to keep him in the public eye were the *Winner's Dinners* column he wrote for *The Sunday Times* — begun in 1984, under the editorship of his friend, Andrew Neil — and his full-time job as a general 'rentaquote' for journalists. I also happened to loathe his films.

After his death, Marc Sinden, the son of Sir Donald Sinden, got in touch to say how, when Winner was directing him in *The Wicked Lady*, he told him to stand in front of a door and 'look surprised' when he opened it. 'Well, I was surprised — there in front of me was a couple actually humping,' said Sinden. 'It took eight takes, and finally the boy ran off leaving this poor girl stark naked. I gave her my coat and asked her "why did you do it?" And she said: "Mr Winner said if I didn't do the scene, I would never work in films again."'

Peter Bowles, meanwhile, related how, after he had alluded in his autobiography to an occasion when a Sloaney girl in Winner's employ had told him that she considered him to be a 'cunt', Winner phoned demanding to know her name. 'I said to him "Michael, it happened forty or fifty years ago, I can't remember." I think he still wanted to have his revenge on her.' Still more revolting stories emerged about Winner and the way he treated women after the Harvey Weinstein scandal. Marina Sirtis, who was directed by Winner in *Death Wish 3*, said what he did to her made her hope he would 'rot in hell for all eternity'.

Michael Winner was born in Hampstead on 30 October 1935, and died in Kensington on 21 January 2013, at the aged of seventy-seven.

Michael Grandage

The first time I remember talking to Michael Grandage was as he was standing anxiously in the foyer of the Donmar Warehouse Theatre in Covent Garden. It was 2006 and the first night of *Frost/Nixon*. 'I've been looking forward to this one,' I said, chirpily. He replied: 'I'm bloody terrified.'

The show turned out to be another of Grandage's triumphs as a director — West End and Broadway transfers ensued and then a film — but his relationship with Frank Langella, whom he'd cast as the disgraced American president, had been challenging, to say the least, and it was no wonder he was ashen-faced. Langella wasn't on speaking terms with his co-star Michael Sheen, who was playing David Frost; he'd eccentrically insisted on being called 'Mr President' backstage; and, feeling his character was being disrespected, had asked that the play's title be changed to Nixon/Frost. It didn't help an already fraught situation that Peter Morgan, its writer, had a habit of talking to Grandage about the actors as if they weren't there.

I'd taken a lofty view of the Donmar when I'd started out as a theatre critic and even remember asking my arts editor if there was any point troubling with a place that could accommodate only 250 souls. He raised his eyes to the heavens. I soon came to understand that, with the right individual in charge, even the tiniest venue can come to dominate theatre land and that was how it was during Grandage's decade as the artistic director of the Donmar.

I look back on my relationship with his theatre as if it were a passionate romance. The first year, I gave it one rave review after another. The second year, I think my hopes were so unrealistically high that they could only possibly be dashed. I took Grandage to lunch at Le Caprice and he wondered why I'd suddenly 'turned'. I replied that he'd caused me to 'recalibrate the meaning of good and bad theatre.' I've no doubt he saw me as an absurdly pretentious pillock, but he understood that I was at least fully engaged and trying to learn, and it was on that basis that we became good friends.

Born in Yorkshire and raised in the West Country, he'd started out, like so many of the greatest directors, as an actor. I happened to see him as a dashingly handsome young man in a rerun of *Rumpole of the Bailey,* playing the boyfriend of the curmudgeonly old barrister's daughter. He demonstrated an exceptional gift for comedy.

His heart was, however, set on being a director and, in 1996, he made his debut in that role at the Mercury Theatre, Colchester, with Arthur Miller's *The Last Yankee.*

Two years later, he was invited by Sheffield Theatres to direct *Twelfth Night*. In the same year, he made his London directorial debut at the Almeida with a production of Shaw's *The Doctor's Dilemma*. He then began a five-year innings as the artistic director at Sheffield Theatres from 2000, where he had some of the brightest and the best queuing up to work for him, including Joseph Fiennes in *Edward II,* Kenneth Branagh in *Richard III,* Diana Rigg in *Suddenly Last Summer* and Derek Jacobi in *The Tempest.*

It doesn't do to over-analyse magic, but Grandage productions always look stunning. His civil partner is the award-winning designer Christopher Oram and I got the impression that when they worked together each scene was composed in their heads as if it was a great classical painting. Grandage always grasped, too, the essential messages of the plays. After *Peter and Alice,* about an encounter between Alice Liddell Hargreaves, the woman who inspired *Alice in Wonderland,* and Peter Llewelyn Davies, one of the boys upon whom Peter Pan was based, I recall him talking with real emotion. 'It's about how we need happy childhoods, as it's those which give us the strength to handle all the pain that inevitably comes our way in later life,' he said. 'Without them, we have no foundations.'

In 2014, he directed his first film, *Genius,* about the relationship between the author Thomas Wolfe and his editor Max Perkins, which starred Colin Firth, Jude Law and Nicole Kidman. Grandage sought artistic rather than overtly commercial success and he achieved it brilliantly. His next big film project is *My Policeman,* based on a novel by Bethan Roberts, with Harry Styles in the starring role. I've talked periodically to Grandage during the lockdowns and he and Oram are the only two people I know who have found in those periods of nothingness a kind of contentment. I suppose it's because they'd never done anything half heartedly that they'd no regrets.

Michael Grandage was born in Yorkshire on 2 May 1962.

Stephen Unwin

Theatres are much like any other places of work and the best directors — like all bosses — create environments in which everyone feels they can succeed. It's all very well to scream at actors and other creatives and generally terrorise them — and this happens — but it's no way to get the best results. Nor, for that matter, does it end well having a vast number of projects on the go at the same time and just popping in every now and again and seeing how things are going.

Stephen Unwin is a perfectionist who grasps very quickly what a play has to say and how it needs to say it. His book *So You Want to be a Theatre Director?* should be required reading, not just for people at all levels within the theatre industry, but anyone setting out to lead any kind of human endeavour. He understands, above all, the human psyche.

I've watched hundreds of plays over the years where I've wondered how on earth they got to be staged with so many things so manifestly wrong with them. So much of it's just about attention to detail or simple good taste, but mostly it's about seeing a show all the time through the eyes of the punters and looking out for their best interests. Unwin knows what does and doesn't make for a good night out at the theatre.

I've seen him at work directing a play and it was fascinating: unobtrusive, almost invisible to start with, he just watched and listened and let everyone do their thing. He understood all about egos and nerves and how

they should be handled, but, slowly, gradually, with a few deft nudges, and often making people think his great ideas had sprung out of their own heads, the thing started to take shape. He reminded me of some of the best news editors I'd worked for, in that he'd never take it upon himself to rewrite a single word, but just ask the playwright 'Are you really sure that works?' Or gently imply that there was a section where it got maybe just a little bit boring. The crucial thing to him was not to waste a theatregoer's time: every second a play runs has to count.

His prodigious talent was obvious right from the start. As a teenager at Downing College, Cambridge, he directed many student productions, including an award-winning *Measure for Measure* that transferred to the Almeida in London, where he was awarded an Arts Council trainee director's bursary. More than fifty professional productions and twelve operas followed. He was the associate director at the Traverse Theatre, Edinburgh, a resident director at the National Theatre Studio and managed to find the time, too, to launch the English Touring Theatre in June 1993.

He succeeded Sir Peter Hall as the artistic director of the Rose Theatre, Kingston, which became a creative powerhouse during his tenure with widely acclaimed productions of *The Winslow Boy* (with Timothy West); *Hay Fever* (Celia Imrie); *The Importance of Being Earnest* and *Farewell to the Theatre* (both with Jane Asher) and a production of *The Lady from the Sea* (Joely Richardson) that he also translated. He's written, too, a profoundly moving trilogy of plays set in the 1930s and 1940s: *All Our Children*, about the Nazi persecution of disabled children; *Poor John*, about John Cornford, the British communist who died aged twenty-one in the Spanish Civil War; and *The Gift*, which focuses on Jewish immigration into Britain in the late 1930s.

It's typical of Unwin that during the lockdowns he used the time constructively and usefully, offering individual acting, directing and writing classes on Zoom. As the father of a youngster with severe learning disabilities, and chair of the KIDS charity, he also campaigned vigorously for vulnerable people not to be overlooked — or, worse, deemed to be second-class citizens — during that challenging time. A photograph he posted on Twitter with his son Joey — the two embraced in a moment of beatific happiness — he captioned ironically with the words: 'So terrible being the dad of a learning disabled son.' It went viral, and, the next morning, I heard him on the *Today* programme eloquently making the point that societies are judged by how they look after their most vulnerable.

It doesn't, of course, follow that such an intensely decent man should also be a great director, but in this case happily it does. I know so many other distinguished directors — including Michael Grandage — who revere him and actors jump at the chance to work with him because he brings out the best in them. Modest and unassuming and determined at all times not to take himself too seriously, I know these lines will embarrass him profoundly, but the man's a star, for all that.

Stephen Unwin was born in Budapest on 29 December 1959.

Indhu Rubasingham

It's hard to put a value on theatre — just as it is on music, football, art or any other endeavour that's prone to become a religion — but a value it undoubtedly has. That was brought home to me after an unusually bleak day at the office.

At the *Daily Telegraph,* we'd gone through one of our periodic management upheavals and ended up with an American internet guru. He'd called us all into a room and told us we needed to up our game. I'd been so incensed by his patronising tone I'd fired off a pearler of an email to him, pointing out a few home truths, that I knew amounted to a suicide note, at least so far as my future on that newspaper was concerned. Still, I'd had enough: the *Telegraph* was beginning what seemed to me a descent into madness.

All set to head home and open a bottle, I remembered I was due to review something called *Handbagged* at the Tricycle in Kilburn in north London. The venue was new to me and its name did little to instil confidence. I was just not in the mood. It was raining torrentially, the tubes were packed and there was a fleeting moment at Victoria Station when I wondered what was the point of it all. On a scale of one to ten, I'd put my morale at minus three.

Within an hour, the curtain had gone up and I was laughing like a howler monkey. *Handbagged*, by Moira Buffini, told the story of Margaret Thatcher's relationship with the Queen and it could have made even a funeral procession fall about with mirth. (A favourite line was

Thatcher saying of Robert Mugabe, with no sense of awareness at all, that 'he's not as black as he's painted'). There was a young actor in it called Neet Mohan who had an exceptional gift for comedy, and the direction by Indhu Rubasingham was sparkling. I got home with my morale up at least eight points.

The next day I did something I'd never done before — or since — and wrote Mohan a fan letter. I asked him to let the whole company know how much they'd cheered me up. I heard back from him that my letter had boosted their morale, too, as it arrived the same day that the theatre critic Quentin Letts had wondered in the *Daily Mail* if there was much point to it. Mohan — now familiar to television viewers in *Casualty* — Letts had described as 'irritating'.

The show made a swift West End transfer and was a big success, and, for a while, played at the same time as *Red Velvet*, another Tricycle production, wowed audiences on Broadway.

Success on this scale for a small theatre in Kilburn was unprecedented, and Rubasingham, the Tricycle's artistic director, began to fascinate me. I took her to lunch —

'please no stuffy club,' she said — and found a woman who was charming, kind and warm, but also fiercely determined to see that her venue continued to punch above its weight.

Nothing had ever been handed to her on a plate: she'd been born in Sheffield to Tamil parents from Sri Lanka, and, after a spell at Nottingham Girls' High School, she'd gone on to study drama at Hull University. There was then an Arts Council bursary to work as an assistant director at the Theatre Royal Stratford East, where Mike Leigh was her boss. She'd then freelanced as a director and I'd caught some of her productions — notably *Disconnect* at the Royal Court, which I'd loved — but it was only after *Handbagged* that I got to appreciate the consistent flair — if not genius — in her work.

She went on to rename her theatre the Kiln — more appealing than the Tricycle, which always put me in mind of something that was rickety and old-fashioned — and then presided over a two-year £7 million refurbishment, which, as bad luck would have it, was completed not long before the coronavirus forced her to plunge her brand new stage into darkness.

Typically, Rubashingham was adamant her theatre would remain relevant during even those grim days and launched an appeal to raise £70,000 to support the venue's community projects, including a collaboration with the charity Food For All to provide free hot meals for homeless people once a week. There was also a project to support youngsters newly arrived in the UK to develop their language skills.

I can't even begin to imagine how hard the lockdowns must have been for her, but this I know — I owe her for lifting my spirits on the most depressing of nights. It thrills me to see that her theatre is once again back in business, lifting the morale of the whole of London.

Indhu Rubasingham was born in Sheffield on 8 February 1970.

Bill Kenwright

Theodore Roosevelt got it about right when he said that it's not the critic who counts, but the man who's actually in the arena. I found myself reflecting on the American president's words when I saw Bill Kenwright in his socially distanced seat at the opening night of his production of *Love Letters*. This was just before Christmas 2020, when theatre was, briefly, legal.

The impresario was, in the all-pervading darkness of the West End, striving valiantly to keep the torch of theatre alight. He had earlier failed — while daring greatly — to stage his novel production of *Hamlet*, with Sir Ian McKellen in the title role, but, undeterred, he then ploughed more money into the plucky Turbine Theatre in south London to help them keep going.

All the other producers were at the time too terrified to put their money where their masked mouths were, but Kenwright has always been bold and his great enthusiasms are life itself to him. There's football and his chairmanship of Everton; the films he's made, such as *The Fanatic* with John Travolta, and *Cheri* with Michelle Pfeiffer; and then the records he has produced under his own label. He has never done anything in his life half-heartedly.

Kenwright is a proud Liverpudlian and he had been at high school in the city at the same time as Paul McCartney and George Harrison. He likes to tell the story of how, at eighteen, he won a place at Manchester University to study English and Drama. His parents couldn't have

Bill Kenwright with his partner, Jenny Seagrove.

been prouder of him, but, as he walked up Deansgate on the way to the university to start his course, something made him turn in the opposite direction, to the Granada Television Studios. There was a sign he saw when he got there saying 'Room 501 — Casting' and he headed to that room, and, affecting to be a young actor of considerable experience and promise, he landed the role of a young office boy in a series called *Villains* on sixty-five guineas a week. Not long after that, he metamorphosed into Gordon Clegg in *Coronation Street* and that was the start of the Bill Kenwright legend.

He then switched from acting and became one of the UK's most successful theatre producers, best known for the long-running West End hit *Blood Brothers* and a record-breaking tour of *Joseph and the Amazing Technicolor Dreamcoat*. Like Lord Delfont, he is an immensely humane businessman. He threw career lifelines to a number of performers going through rough times — David Cassidy, among them — and he offered Robert Vaughn, then in his eighties, his final stage role in *Twelve Angry Men*. It meant the world to Vaughn to tread the boards one last time, even though it was sometimes a lottery whether he would, as the senior juror, come out with a guilty or not guilty verdict. Kenwright came to the aid, too, of Kenneth Williams, who wrote about him in his *Diaries* with gratitude and affection.

Kenwright told me once: 'Those who know me really well know that at heart I'm a shy man. I play the part I choose to play as well as I can. I'm helped hugely by special people — not least my partner Jenny (Seagrove) — and special friends. My mum always taught me that I would dine with princes and paupers and find they're basically the same, and that, above all things, I must never give up on Hope, as that happened to be her name.'

Of 2020, he admitted: 'It's been a horrible year. Like most of us, I've lost friends and seen so many struggling. I've even seen actors give up their lives out of an inability to see a future. We all try to be cheerful, but ebullience always comes with times of doubt and loss.'

The tumultuous applause at the end of the first night of *Love Letters* was, I felt, as much for Kenwright as it was for the players, and, needless to say, he brought the play back the moment he was allowed, and, a few months later, the Ian McKellen *Hamlet*. Putting a brave face on a bloody awful time, he joked: 'As we were saying, before we were so rudely interrupted...'

Bill Kenwright was born in Liverpool on 4 September 1945.

Peter Ustinov

I f ever there was a model European, it was Sir Peter Ustinov. It was while working for the first *European* newspaper — the one launched by Robert Maxwell in 1990 — that I got to know him. Maxwell may have thought of Ustinov as his friend, but Ustinov saw through the old rogue. Indeed, he confided in me that he saw Maxwell as 'a larger-than-life actor who'd simply got in over his head'. Still, he took Maxwell seriously when he suggested he write a column for his brand new newspaper for the whole of Europe.

He dutifully turned out for *The European*'s big London launch party at the Connaught Rooms to listen to Maxwell's speech — a curious mixture of idealism and bombast — alongside the former prime minister James Callaghan and the then Labour leader Neil Kinnock (who'd managed to pull strings to get his children, Stephen and Rachel, work experience jobs in the newsroom).

Of course, Ustinov's reputation preceded him — as a writer, an intellectual and a diplomat, as well as an Oscar-winning actor — but he approached his first job in journalism with endearing humility. He'd always file *Ustinov at Large* early so that — in his words — 'the editor could check it was all right'. He wrote it in a peculiarly self-deprecating style. 'That I'm inexperienced in the field of journalism is self-evident, but I am eager and learning fast,' he began an early column.

In his trepidation, Ustinov reminded me of myself starting out, as an anxious teenager, on my first local newspaper. I had been dazzled by the wit he'd displayed in his books, plays and chat show appearances, but his column turned out to be unexpectedly heavy going. He'd write for us as he travelled the world, often filing from film sets and international conferences, but seldom, if ever, were his columns anywhere near as funny or perceptive as he was in person.

He just didn't understand what made good copy. It didn't occur to him, for instance, to write a column about his seventieth birthday party at the UNESCO building in Paris, where Sir Yehudi Menuhin, Larry Adler and Sir Edward Heath provided the music. A piece about that had to be cobbled together for us at the last minute by a staff reporter using photographs that had come in from the wire services.

None of us dared to talk through with Ustinov what it was that made a column readable, and he, in turn, was trying too hard, agonising over every syllable. He seemed, too, to be in awe of newspapers and to be labouring under a misapprehension about the size of our readership: photographs of unsold copies of the original *European* had become a running joke in *Private Eye*. Oblivious, Ustinov kept tapping away, week in, week out. 'One of the wonderful privileges in having a column of newsprint at your disposal is that it enables you to write suggestions,' Ustinov wrote quaintly in another column.

European unity mattered to Ustinov and indeed he embodied it. He had Italian, Polish, French and German blood running through his veins — in addition to the blood of a number of non-European countries — and I doubt any man had ever assembled a more cosmopolitan collection of friends than he had. He seemed congenitally incapable of not liking anyone. As a private in the army, he had seen at first hand the devastation of the Second World War and so he understood better than most what ensued when people — and countries — decided to go it alone.

Looking back, we should have just got him to write about his film career, which he loved to talk about. He

Peter Ustinov in *Spartacus* (1960) for which he won an Oscar.

had an extraordinary talent for oral and physical mimicry and an unerring eye for detail. My favourite anecdote was how he'd gone to a reading for the film *Spartacus* when Laurence Olivier had sneakily persuaded its star and producer Kirk Douglas to extend his part at the expense of Charles Laughton's. Ustinov captured with absolute perfection the look of fury on Laughton's face — and the fury, too, in his voice — when he realised exactly what Olivier had been up to.

Ustinov wrote in one of his last columns how he was 'determined to use the privilege of being able to say what I have on my mind in this column while I still have it'. He seemed to sense the game was almost up. In 1991, after Maxwell went over the side of his yacht in mysterious circumstances, the controlling Mirror Group decided it

was time to jettison the loss-making paper and call in the administrators. The entire *European* staff agreed to write for nothing for a month while new owners were sought.

My phone went just after it had been put to a vote and it was Ustinov. I told him we couldn't pay him, but he said without hesitation that he would keep furnishing us with columns so long as we could furnish him with the space. I don't necessarily say he was the greatest journalist I ever worked with, but it still makes me proud to think that this charming and generous man was once my colleague.

Sir Peter Ustinov, born in London on 16 April 1921, and died in Genolier, Switzerland, on 28 March 2004 at the age of eighty-two.

Frances Barber

It was a young man named Tyler who first acquainted me with Frances Barber. She boarded a plane at Heathrow bound for Los Angeles and he'd been seated beside her. The crew made a big fuss of the actress and brought her champagne, even though she was travelling economy. She was at the time appearing in the prime-time television series *Silk*.

She'd introduced herself to Tyler, but he was preoccupied with storing his flute and seemed to be in a world of his own. With no one to talk to, and take off delayed, she live-tweeted her bemusement. 'Tyler is the worst companion on a flight, ever,' she harrumphed. 'The purser asked if it was me, from *Silk*, but Tyler didn't ask me a single, solitary thing. You'd think he might wonder what I did? Oh no.'

I managed to track down Tyler and the story got better and better. He turned out to be not just a musician, but also a professional contortionist and said he'd been totally unaware of what he called his fellow passenger's 'need for validation'. I ran a piece in the *Daily Telegraph* diary along the lines of 'actress couldn't cope with being ignored', and illustrated it with a picture of Tyler showing off his considerable skills as a contortionist.

The next time I had cause to write about Frances was when I reviewed her in the title role of an all-female production of *Julius Caesar* at the Donmar in Covent Garden. I didn't care for it, and, in my notice, I gave Frances a stabbing that was every bit as brutal as she'd received on stage.

It was nothing personal, of course, but it's fair to say, what with one thing and another, I didn't anticipate us ever becoming great friends. I had not, however, reckoned with the EU referendum campaign, which had the curious effect of turning some of my friends into enemies and some enemies into friends. Happily, Frances fell into the latter category.

On Twitter, I saw an obvious patriotism in what she was writing. We both shared an idea of what our country should be about and we saw in Brexit and the people propagating it just about everything that was alien to that idea. She followed me and I followed her back and I direct-messaged her to say I was sorry I'd been such a shit. She was only too willing to forgive my foolish ways.

She'd been a Labour supporter all her life, but was, during that period, in despair about Jeremy Corbyn. I was at the time beginning a brief and ill-starred fling with the Lib Dems, and, when there was a by-election in Lewisham East, not long after the referendum, I suggested she come and campaign with the candidate Lucy Salek and the then party leader Sir Vince Cable and I could write about it for *The New European.*

She was appearing on the West End stage with the Brexit-supporting Edward Fox in *An Ideal Husband,* but she gamely agreed. I suggested we board the Thames Clipper at Embankment — close to her theatre — voyage to Greenwich and get a cab from there. She arrived at the jetty in a vast summer hat and sunglasses and looked, for all the world, like Greta Garbo.

I have no idea what Sir Vince made of us, but it made for an entertaining piece. I subsequently had Frances over to dinner and we saw each other at a few first nights and I grew to admire and revere her. She lights up a room when she walks into it — all those hilarious theatrical anecdotes and that infectious, throaty laugh — but there's a social conscience there, too, and a fearlessness that made her a hate figure among Corbyn's legions of keyboard warriors.

We never had to talk about the Lib Dems, but our disillusionment with the party under Jo Swinson kept to the same tramlines and we both came to pin our hopes on Labour. Two things I can now say for sure — Frances is a lot more fun to have as a friend than as an enemy. And, as for Tyler, he did himself no favours on that flight. For the lady seated beside him, he should have bent over backwards.

Frances Barber was born in Wolverhampton on 13 May 1958.

Sarah Miles

S arah Miles and I should really be friends. I spent what was — at least until the last half hour — a blissfully happy day at her eleventh century manor house in the Sussex countryside. The actress, best known for *Those Magnificent Men in their Flying Machines, The Servant* and *Hope and Glory*, made me an impromptu lunch, challenged me to a game of table tennis (which I ungallantly won), and then, in the afternoon, showed me the spot on her croquet lawn where her husband Robert Bolt had been buried.

We'd first met in 1988 when she'd been appearing in a play called *Asylum* at the Lyric Theatre in Hammersmith, west London. She was then a morose and distracted interviewee. It was perhaps not surprising as she was caring for Bolt — the man who wrote *A Man for All Seasons* — after his debilitating stroke in 1979 and she was trying to make ends meet. The Sarah I caught up with at her home — twenty-one years after Bolt's death — seemed more at ease with herself. She was into star signs and seemed reassured when I said I was a Cancerian.

Our meeting had followed a lengthy exchange of emails in which she mainly wanted to establish that I wouldn't raise the issue of her drinking her own urine, which was a matter that featured heavily in her press cuttings. For the record, it's true, she does, but she swears that it has health benefits.

She was a fount, too, of showbiz gossip. Her late husband had also written the screenplay to *Ryan's Daughter*, in

which she'd starred, and she said everyone was appalled when John Mills had arrived on the set with his hair cut brutally short and his face distorted by fearsome false teeth and padding. 'Nobody had asked John to do that. His performance as that mute village idiot ended up winning him an Oscar, but his characterisation wasn't what Robert had had in mind at all. We could all see only too well that he was just showing off, terribly.'

Sarah talked, too, of her languidly handsome co-star Christopher Jones, whom she recalled later encountering by chance, not long before his death in 2014, in Los Angeles. 'He had succumbed to various addictions, looked like a long-haired old tramp, and, after following me around, exposed himself to me in a lift.' Then there were her relationships. Laurence Olivier she described as 'a complicated man who seemed to be jealous of Ralph Richardson because he could communicate an innocence in his acting that he knew he could never manage'. She'd loved, too, Steven Spielberg and her *Ryan's Daughter* co-star Robert Mitchum, and we'd discussed their insecurities, and Trevor Howard's 'epic drinking sessions' during the making of *White Mischief,* when she'd done her best to protect him from himself.

It was late into the afternoon when politics finally brought our conversation to a juddering halt. The EU referendum was then four months away and I hadn't planned raising it with her as it had seemed to me at the time a foregone conclusion, and, anyway, this was a showbiz interview. Sarah asked me how I was going to vote and was dismayed when I made it clear I was a Remainer. Suddenly she was saying I was 'an Establishment man, dull, boring, unable to think outside of the box'.

She told me she was thinking about touring the country to try to rally people to her cause and had not only written a poem about Brexit, but also a song with the repeated refrain 'C'mon, old England'. I sat quietly as she belted out all five verses. I respected Sarah as an actress, and still do, but on this issue she startled me. She was, looking back, the first supporter of Brexit I'd ever met. It was a jolt that made me suddenly aware the ground I was standing on wasn't nearly as stable as I'd imagined.

Sometimes, it's best to keep shtum — I was her guest, after all — but, with Sarah, I was simply not prepared to go with the flow. We parted rather formally, both sensing we'd be unlikely to see each other ever again.

Sarah Miles was born on 31 December 1941, in Ingatestone, Essex.

Sarah Miles with her late husband, the screenwriter, Robert Bolt.

Hugh Grant

Hounds chase foxes not out of any personal antipathy, but because it's what their lords and masters train them to do. It was once a bit like that between Hugh Grant and me.

The stand the actor has taken on media intrusion into people's lives — including his own — meant he was considered to be legitimate prey by at least one of my former employers. The feeling was that he had to be put in his place. If he were allowed to get his way and new privacy laws were to be introduced, then the press would be further fettered and individuals a lot more powerful than him would be able to use them to shield their nefarious activities.

Still, I remember feeling guilt as I watched Grant give evidence to the Leveson inquiry into ethics in my industry and realised how miserable his life had been made. His phone had been hacked, the paparazzi hounded him and those he loved, his medical records were once leaked, what free time he had was largely spent on libel actions, and he had, too, to be on constant lookout for paid informants, including even in hospitals and among the police officers he'd occasionally have to turn to for help.

As much as we in newspapers like to present our readers with a world of heroes and villains, it's seldom, of course, that simple. I've got to know Grant well enough over the past few years to be remorseful about how I used to write about him. He's a decent, principled and forgiving man — and, of course, a wonderful actor. I've grown up with his

films — from the breezy optimism of *Four Weddings and a Funeral, Notting Hill* and *Love Actually* to the mature and haunting portrayal of Jeremy Thorpe and the glorious send-up of himself in *Paddington 2*.

It's the off-screen Grant that has, however, come to impress me the most. Actors are generally advised by their PR people not to talk about politics — let alone an issue as contentious as Brexit — as it runs the risk of alienating fans and even casting directors. Grant couldn't care less and I saw in what he said on this issue — and in his campaigning for pro-EU candidates in marginal seats in the 2019 election — a crystal clear patriotism. I know he has also put his money where his mouth is in terms of helping some individuals involved in the European cause, and all this has inevitably made him even more of a hate figure among the Brexit-backing newspaper proprietors.

Hugh Grant told Sarah Vine and her former husband, Michael Gove, where to get off in two brief words.

There's a limit, however, to how far Grant is willing to be pushed. At a party, he was approached by Sarah Vine and her then husband Michael Gove. Savaged that very morning by Vine in her *Daily Mail* column, he told them where to get off. The two-word put-down won him a spontaneous round of applause from fellow guests.

After I watched a rerun of the ITV drama *The Lost Honour of Christopher Jefferies* — which related how the press turned a retired and totally innocent schoolmaster into a national hate figure following the murder of Joanna Yeates — I messaged Grant to say I felt it showed how his had been a brave and necessary campaign. He said it had often got lonely and my words had touched him.

The argument that the press wouldn't be able to stop the rich and powerful from misbehaving doesn't really hold so much sway now. They are misbehaving and a lot of newspapers don't appear to care. Worse, it has often been the newspapers themselves that have been misbehaving. My industry's collective behaviour over the past few years has lost us the moral high ground.

Actors aren't, of course, supposed to know more than journalists, but I'd say this one knows more than most of us. He understands, too, 'the British sense of decency' — a phrase he used to great effect at the Leveson inquiry — and he can see the good in people as well as the bad. Grant is a fine actor, but also, and more importantly, a principled and fully-paid-up human being. 'I really do feel,' he once said to me, 'that we have to be better than this.'

Hugh Grant was born in White City, London, on 9 September 1960.

Hugh Grant played the role of Jeremy Thorpe in the BBC drama *A Very English Scandal* (2018).

Patrick Stewart

E ver since he first stood with a placard bearing the name of his local Labour candidate in Mirfield in the West Riding of Yorkshire in the 1945 general election — at the age of just five — Sir Patrick Stewart has been a steadfast member of the party. The distinguished actor duly spoke up for Jeremy Corbyn when he was elected leader and backed him in the first general election he fought, even if, in private, he was becoming, in common with a great many Labour members, frustrated over his position on Brexit.

Then he saw Corbyn in the flesh one night and thought he'd bend his ear. 'He was talking to a group of my friends after a theatre performance and I wandered up. Jeremy's eye caught mine and he said "oh, you're looking very well", and I made some light-hearted riposte along the lines of "you can't judge a book by its cover." For some inexplicable reason, this annoyed him, and he shot back "you know, Patrick, you could just have said thank you, instead of making a joke out of it." I couldn't understand how he could take offence at such an innocuous remark, and no one else could, and it made for an awkward silence. I just thought "oh well, I tried," and, after a suitable interval, I discreetly headed off home.'

The encounter symbolised the pretty pass that the distinguished Shakespearean actor — lately best known as Jean-Luc Picard in the Star Trek films — had reached in his relationship with the Labour Party. When I met him at his flat overlooking Hyde Park in London in the

summer of 2018, I asked if he would be voting for the party at the next general election if Corbyn still led it. After an anguished pause, he said probably not, if it still supported Brexit and was unable to deal with such obvious evils in its midst as anti-Semitism.

In an unnervingly McCarthyite time, Sir Patrick refused to be browbeaten into keeping his thoughts on Brexit to himself, and, predictably, the interview I did with him for *The New European* resulted in online abuse — even threats of violence — but he was unperturbed. 'Friends have asked if it's sensible to get into all of this publicly, but I'm seventy-eight now and I think a lot about the kind of world my children and grandchildren will be left with and it worries me. I've had a chance to make something of my life and I want that for them, too. I'm also a war baby — I was very aware, growing up, that families around me had lost people they loved and often depended upon — and the EU always seemed to me to offer a way to ensure peace and stability in this increasingly uncertain world of ours.'

For all that he had achieved in his life, Sir Patrick was in person humble, unassuming and sensitive. It hurt that the right-wing press portrayed him as a 'Remainer luvvie', who jetted in occasionally from Los Angeles to lecture the

British public. He happened to be very much a Londoner and his background hardly fitted in with that notion — Dad was a sergeant major in the army, Mum worked in a textile mill and money was in short supply as he was growing up — but he could see what was going on. 'There is a new kind of anger and irrationality that Brexit has given expression to, but I will not be intimidated.

'I never set out to be a celebrity, but it came unexpectedly, relatively late, after *Star Trek: The Next Generation* first aired, and I realised it brings with it certain responsibilities. I've talked to Ian McKellen and others about this, and, as pompous as this may sound, I think a lot of us in the entertainment business feel we should try to do what we can to make the world a better place. Ian is a serious activist on gay rights and so many issues and I would never compare myself to him, but I do what I can. It startles me the influence that people like me can have on social media and so on.'

Sir Patrick inevitably detested Donald Trump and was conscious that what he was trying to do was to normalise offensiveness. 'We are getting used to this technique now, where a politician without any scruples says the great big lie or outrageous thing and it gets all the headlines, and then, if someone manages to prove it's made up, there's maybe a retraction of some kind that goes in small type on an inside page and no one notices. We're seeing this here, too. People said after Boris Johnson talked about Muslim women "going around looking like letterboxes or bank robbers" that he was just joking and it was only "Boris being Boris", but no, actually, it was not all right. It was insulting and discriminating and anyone who knows anything about history knows where that can lead.'

He saw Brexit and Trump and the rise of maverick politicians around the world as the inevitable consequence of a divide that was allowed to open up between elected representatives and those who elected them. 'There were people who saw this sense of alienation and exploited it and we have now this politics of selfishness — where it's all about this idea we are taking care of ourselves and to hell with everyone else — but we have so many issues now that are confronting us, such as automation, and, even more importantly, climate change, that we have to work out how to tackle together. This is no time for isolationism. I have nightmarish visions, of course, about where we are headed now. It can only really take us to a place where the very rich withdraw behind security gates and barbed wire fences and we give up on the idea of the kind of community I've known all my life. I am not, however, reconciled to this in any way at all. I sense more and more we are seeing this and recoiling from it.'

Sir Patrick has always been at heart an optimist, and, while he knew a lot of damage had already been done to Britain by the Brexiters, he had no doubt that the country would eventually recover. 'I think we will come out of this experience a lot stronger. We have all of us learnt from it. I think it will make us appreciate basic freedoms and rights that perhaps in the past we took too much for granted. I think we will look back on it as a turning point in our history.'

Sir Patrick Stewart was born in the West Riding of Yorkshire on 13 July 1940.

Ian McDiarmid

For a very decent man, Ian McDiarmid has turned out to be very good at playing wicked men. The Emperor Palpatine in the Star Wars films, a psychopathic con man in *Inspector Morse* and even Satan himself in a BBC Radio 4 dramatisation of John Milton's *Paradise Lost*. The most challenging role of them all was, however, Enoch Powell in the play *What Shadows* that was first performed in Birmingham — where the politician delivered his 'rivers of blood' speech — a few months after the Brexit vote.

'I knew it could be dangerous, but there are so many facets to Powell's character that the challenge he offered to me as an actor was irresistible,' said McDiarmid. 'There is an epic Shakespearean sweep to his rise and fall and it's hard not to see echoes of *Coriolanus*. The way Chris Hannan has written the piece is, however, not judgemental. We leave it to audiences to judge.'

The actor didn't share Powell's views on race and he voted Remain in the EU referendum — but he was struck by how little had really changed in the country in terms of the underlying fears and insularity. I saw the play first in Birmingham, and, again, when McDiarmid brought it to London, the following year. Its dramatic highpoint was inevitably when Powell quoted Sibyl's prophecy in Virgil's epic poem the *Aeneid*. 'As I look ahead, I am filled with foreboding. Like the Roman, I see "the River Tiber foaming with much blood".

'That speech packs a punch for young people who haven't heard it, and I think it often depresses the older ones as it shows how little we've moved on,' said McDiarmid. 'The point Powell made about race is now being made by Nigel Farage and others like him — but without, of course, Powell's intellectual hinterland. He was, above all things, an emotional man, and it is his emotional core that drives the piece — hence the title, which comes from Edmund Burke's line: "What shadows we are and what shadows we pursue".'

The play focused on Powell's doomed friendship with Clem Jones, the liberal-minded editor of the *Express and Star* newspaper in his Wolverhampton constituency. Powell consulted him in advance on how to attract media attention for his big speech, but did not divulge its contents. The actor met the late Clem Jones's journalist son, Nicholas. 'I felt a bit self-conscious about the poetic way we showed his father picnicking with Powell and the two of them making long, flowery speeches. "I was there on those picnics," Nick told me. "I'm afraid it was even worse than that — Enoch orated to trees".'

As an actor, McDiarmid felt he had an overriding responsibility to Powell himself, who was not around to defend himself — and also to his two surviving children

— Susan and Jennifer. 'I was asked if we should invite them to see the play, but I felt we should leave it to them,' he said. 'I suspect the last thing they'd want is to have to relive that time again.'

McDiarmid was twenty-four and at acting school in Glasgow when Powell made that speech in the spring of 1968, and, of course, like everyone in the country he was aware of the impact it had. 'I had an image of Powell then as the big, bad wolf but, when I started to research this role — reading the books and seeing the newsreel footage — I realised we had things in common. He was something of an actor himself in many ways. He valued logic and reason, and he had the quality of authenticity. It would have appalled him the way politicians now all too often say things that they know to be untrue.'

The play attracted all ethnicities, and white members of the audiences had talked to McDiarmid about feeling 'awkward' during some scenes. 'Theatre shouldn't always make you feel comfortable,' McDiarmid said. 'It should be challenging sometimes.' He said the awkwardness never extended to the rehearsal room, where his fellow cast members — including the superb Waleed Akhtar of the film *Salmon Fishing in the Yemen* — could discuss the issues the play raised intelligently and dispassionately.

McDiarmid had been made to look uncannily like the character. He had grown a pencil moustache for the part and the wig designer Richard Mawbey had gifted him a perfect Powellian quiff. The actor even spent time with Parkinson's sufferers to help him to understand how best to portray the condition that afflicted the politician in his later years. The result was unnervingly true to the original, but McDiarmid would not accept that he had reanimated a monster. 'We have to face up to our past and talk it through,' he said. 'Part of that, I think, is getting our heads around Powell. We need to face down all of our demons.'

Ian McDiarmid was born in Angus, Scotland, on 11 August 1944.

Bernard Delfont

L ord Delfont has enjoyed something of a career renaissance in recent years, albeit posthumously. Sir Michael Gambon played the great show business impresario as a thoroughly decent man in the film *Judy* — the Judy Garland biopic that had Renée Zellweger in the title role — and, the year before that, there was *Stan & Ollie*, in which Rufus Jones also got across his generosity of spirit as he fixed a British tour for the comedy duo in their twilight years.

I met Delfont in 1986 when, despite the fact he was seventy-seven, he was energetically chairing the entertainment conglomerate First Leisure. For all that he'd achieved, he was every bit as warm, charming and modest as the two recent film portrayals suggested and insisted on me calling him Bernard. 'Sir Bernard sounded a lot friendlier. I hardly get the time to go to the debates in the House, and, anyway, it was all luck so what's the point making a fuss about it?'

I was just a callow local newspaper reporter who'd come up from the sticks to interview him, but he treated me like a member of the Windsor family at The Royal Variety Show, and, even as his secretary kept buzzing through to remind him of other commitments in his diary, he allowed me to go on well into extra time.

It wasn't just Judy Garland and Laurel and Hardy who owed him, but a whole generation of stars that he'd helped on their way, among them Morecambe and Wise, Tommy Steele, Danny La Rue, Frankie Howerd, Norman Wisdom

Bernard Delfont (left) with his brother, Lew Grade.

and Tommy Cooper. He'd also, in his previous role at EMI, overseen what for my money were two of the most stylish and opulent films ever made: the Albert Finney *Murder on the Orient Express* and the Peter Ustinov *Death on the Nile.* This was a man who'd helped to entertain us all at some point in our lives.

Delfont had experienced poverty and misery in his life, as well as wealth and success, and it was almost certainly that which made him so grounded. He'd been born in Tokmak, a poverty-stricken village in what was then still the Russian Empire, the second son of Isaac and Olga Winogradsky. In 1912, the family fled the pogroms and ended up living in the East End of London. Mindful of the more subtle anti-Semitism that was then prevalent in England, they Anglicised their names and began what turned out to be three remarkable careers.

'There is something about people who come to this country with no money,' Delfont told me. 'They often go far because they are prepared to work hard, prepared to give more of themselves. They are people who know how privileged they are.'

His brother Leslie became probably the most celebrated theatrical agent of his day, with the likes of Laurence Olivier and Danny Kaye on his books. He is the father of Michael — now Lord — Grade, the television executive and businessman. The third Winogradsky brother was Lord Lew Grade, the film and television mogul. 'People say Lew and I run show business together, but it's not quite like that,' Delfont said. 'I may be Lew's brother, but in business, believe me, we're at each other's throats.'

He admitted there had been terrible rows over the years, not least when they both found themselves making rival films about the very same subject. 'Lew was making *Raise the Titanic* at the same time that my organisation was filming *SOS Titanic*. It was dreadful timing, but, by the time we found out what the other was up to, it was too late for either of us to change course.' Both films sank without trace and Lew famously observed, when he looked at the profit and loss accounts for *Raise the Titanic*, that it would have been 'cheaper to have lowered the Atlantic'.

When we had met, Delfont was still mourning his mother Olga, who had died at the age of ninety-six. That loss had, he said, brought him and Lew closer together. It was just the two of them by then: Leslie had died in 1979 after a long period of ill health at just sixty-three.

I asked Delfont if he had any plans to retire to his country house in Angmering in West Sussex and he laughed. 'I'm a grafter and grafters don't quit,' he said. Delfont was to graft for another seven years and Lew for twelve. I remember Delfont vividly because, as an immigrant, he appreciated this country so very much. 'I've always thought of it as a privilege to live here, not a right,' he said.

Lord Delfont was born in Tokmak in Ukraine in the former Russian Empire on 5 September 1909, and died on 28 July 1994, at the age of eighty-four.

Susannah York

I thought when I was younger that I had a God-given right to happiness, but now I see that no one has,' Susannah York told me. 'I've taken a lot of risks in my life, personally as well as professionally. Some people would say I've been foolhardy, and a lot of the time I would agree with them, but at least I've tried.'

It was the late 1990s and York — fiftysomething, but still stunningly beautiful — was taking a break from rehearsals for a production of *Hamlet* at the Barbican in London and reflecting upon her eventful life. She was conscious that she was an actress upon whom most people had formed an opinion of one kind or another.

Some saw her as that meddlesome luvvie who spouted off all the time about her pet causes, such as CND, rainforests or Israel's prisoner of conscience, Mordechai Vanunu. Others looked upon her as one of the great 'English rose' actresses: fresh-faced, a bit reserved, but utterly compelling in all the diverse parts she had played. And, so far as the readers of the gossip columns were concerned, she was a cougar who, since her marriage to the writer Michael Wells had ended, kept dating men young enough to be her sons.

A feminist in the days when that took courage, she resented it when she saw mention of her 'toyboys'. 'I mean, if I were a man who went out with younger women, it simply wouldn't be commented upon, but it's different for a woman. There are so many attitudes we have in this country that are inherently sexist.' York took a stand

when she realised, making the television series *Trainer*, that her male colleagues Nigel Davenport and David McCallum were both being paid twenty-five per cent more than her. 'I got top billing, but not top pay. That was an issue within the acting profession that needed to be raised and so I had no hesitation in raising it.'

She had always felt injustice keenly. On the set of *Freud*, she was appalled at the way the film's director John Huston relentlessly bullied Montgomery Clift. 'John was continually rewriting scenes that Clift had already learned and making him play them in painfully long takes, with hundreds of extras watching. It was inevitable that Monty and John would not get on, not least because Monty was gay and John so very macho. I stuck up for Monty, but it was difficult coming between them because, if John was a sadist, then Monty was a masochist.'

She found herself, too, in the middle of a bitter feud between Coral Browne and Beryl Reid when they played her rival lesbian lovers in the film *The Killing of Sister George*. 'They both saw me as someone they could speak to, as they didn't find it easy speaking to each other. Coral would phone most mornings very early before filming and grumble for twenty minutes. It took me a while to realise that I could leave the phone on the table and get on with my breakfast, just saying "yes" every now and again, because she only did monologues. She could be very caustic, and Beryl was waspish sometimes, but they both had their hearts in absolutely the right place.'

She was inevitably not a huge fan of Charlton Heston, her co-star in a dire horror film called *The Awakening*. 'I agreed with Charlton on absolutely nothing, but, to be fair, he always treated me with a certain old-world courtesy,' she said. 'I'd thought, when I'd read the script to that film, it was going to be a spoof, but, on the first day of filming, I realised it was all in deadly earnest, and, of course, Charlton had absolutely no sense of humour whatsoever.'

Marlon Brando, meanwhile, 'shocked' her, as he had Harry Andrews, when he arrived on the *Superman* set to perform his brief cameo and it became clear that he hadn't bothered to learn his lines, even though he was commanding a fee of several million dollars. York pocketed just $20,000 for her role as Superman's mum, but, conscious of what Brando had achieved in his career, she couldn't, in that instance, complain. 'They were paying for the legend,' she said. 'When we weren't filming, I found it impossible not to like Marlon. He was brilliant and funny and down to earth.'

In 1973, York wrote a children's book called *In Search of Unicorns*, about the special things that people search for in their lives. I asked her if she felt she had ever found her own unicorn. She thought for a few moments. 'In the book, the heroine discovers that sometimes you find your unicorn and then you lose it. Sometimes it comes back of its own accord and sometimes your unicorn can change. I think I've come to all of those points in my life so far, and perhaps I'll revisit them again...'

Susannah York was born in Chelsea on 9 January 1939, and died in the same London borough on 15 January 2011, aged seventy-two.

Dora Bryan

ora Bryan was resolutely cheerful, unpretentious and as British as fish and chips. She ran a rambling hotel on Brighton seafront with her husband Bill and would, more often than not, be dashing to make the train to London to appear on the West End stage.

When I interviewed her in the 1980s, she was starring in two shows simultaneously: *The Apple Cart,* alongside Peter O'Toole, and the musical *Charlie Girl*, with Cyd Charisse. Her exits and entrances in the productions required split-second timing and costume changes and waiting cabs, and how she managed both curtain calls was a nightly miracle. Even when there were no delays on British Rail, she would seldom make it home to bed much before two a.m.

She had in her day appeared in classic films such as *A Taste of Honey, The Blue Lamp* and *The Fallen Idol.* Noël Coward had given her the big break: he'd spotted her in rep and cast her in *Private Lives* and persuaded her to change her surname from Broadbent to Bryan as he reckoned it was a bit more theatrical.

The word that Coward used to describe the lass from Oldham was 'warm' and that's how I remember her. In those days, I'd lived not far from her hotel and had got used to seeing her on the seafront. One morning, I introduced myself and suggested she talk to me for the *Evening Argus*. There was no standing on ceremony: she suggested a meeting that afternoon.

I arrived to find her in an animated discussion with a plumber, a guest who couldn't get hot water and Bill, whose trousers were water-soaked, and, once she'd sorted all of that out, she got me a cuppa and sat me in what she called — good Lancashire lass that she always was — her 'front room'. She didn't seem remotely like an actress and that, she said, had been one of her problems.

'I'm sure I could have got a lot more money — and maybe more awards — if I'd spent more time creating a bit of an aura around myself, but, you see, my parents were down to earth and they would never have stood for any of that malarkey. The other problem I've had with my life is that reality keeps butting in. I lost two of my babies, survived a horrific car crash, in Spain, and our

Dora Bryan with Juliette Kaplan (left) in the BBC comedy series
Last of the Summer Wine (1973–2010).

son Daniel has been struck by a rare arthritic condition called ankylosing spondylitis. I've also had two nervous breakdowns and joined Alcoholics Anonymous.'

This sort of honesty about mental health was rare when we were speaking, but she said she'd been brought up to be honest. She wondered sometimes if she wasn't 'too sensitive' to be an actress. The critic Bernard Levin had made her burst into tears when he had called her 'grotesque' in a review of one of her early stage performances. 'I've always tried my best. My father owned a small mill that went bankrupt and he was forced to sell bobbins door-to-door and sometimes he'd take me with him. It wasn't his fault what happened, but it gave me a taste of failure early on and it terrified me.'

She was in her mid-sixties when we'd met, tanned and full of life, but, when I'd asked her about the future, she suddenly looked worried. She said she 'hoped for the best'. It wasn't until 1996 that she was finally honoured — an OBE, but it should have been a DBE — and, in the same year, she won an Olivier Award for her role in *The Birthday Party*. Parts in *Last of the Summer Wine,*

Dinnerladies and *Absolutely Fabulous* kept her name in lights, but her last years weren't easy. She had to nurse Bill thorough Alzheimer's and they'd had to sell the hotel because of bankruptcy, and — increasingly frail after her husband died in 2008 — she'd ended up in a nursing home in Hove. She died, aged ninety-one, six years later.

Dora Bryan was born in Southport, Lancashire, on 7 February 1923, and died in Hove in Sussex on 23 July 2014.

Vera Lynn

When it was said how wonderfully the Queen had uttered the words 'we'll meet again' during her address to the nation as it prepared to go into the first lockdown, one woman would have had every reason to take umbrage. Dame Vera Lynn made them her own in innumerable concerts and a radio programme called *Sincerely Yours* that was broadcast to the troops during the war.

Dame Vera was, of course, far too demure to raise so much as a well-plucked eyebrow. And, anyway, it's not as if the words were holy writ. 'I remember when I first saw them on a song sheet, and thought, "well, they've a certain ring to them," but not for one moment did I think I'd still be singing them decades on and they'd still mean so much to people.'

She had seen other songs come and go — and other singers — and recognised what a help it had been for her career to have become so indelibly associated with a great victory. 'Singers today haven't got anything like that to hang on to and all too often get forgotten. It was my good fortune to be singing the right songs at the right time.'

I met Dame Vera in 1986 at her home in Ditchling in the rolling Sussex Downs, and, at the time, the country was getting on with life, and its politicians — a lot of them having served in the war — saw no reason to keep dwelling on it. Indeed, it was even becoming fashionable in some quarters to question a lot of what had happened. A book called *The 1945 Revolution* by William Harrington and Peter

Young had provocatively claimed that 'the sentimental sloppy muck' put out by Dame Vera in *Sincerely Yours* — broadcast between 1941 and 1942 and listened to on Sunday nights by twenty per cent of the population — had contributed to Labour's landslide victory over Churchill in 1945. 'Really,' Dame Vera said, aghast that I should have raised it. 'If any of that were true, I wouldn't be in such demand from ex-servicemen's organisations. And to say *Sincerely Yours* was political docsn't make sense. The war rendered party politics irrelevant.'

Dame Vera made it a rule then — and kcpt to it, until her dying day — never to talk politics. She always knew her own mind, however, and I was interested to find out to what extent her husband Harry Lewis, a clarinetist and saxophonist whom she'd married in 1941, had been a motivating force for her during the war years. 'Obviously the fact I was married to someone who was Jewish gave me a particular horror of the Nazis. Just before the war began, I did a show for Jewish children to raise money to bring them to Britain for refuge. It seemed like the least I could do.'

She had twice retired from show business, first in 1946, then in 1952 — each time it was to get on with her own life — but, when I met her thirty-four years ago, she had reconciled herself to being in a state of 'perpetual semi-retirement'. The Forces had had their flirtations with famous pin-ups, but it was Dame Vera who became their sweetheart because she embodied the enduring British virtues: decency, level-headedness and quiet determination.

She took seriously her role in life and said she was aware she had to live up to a certain ideal. 'I've always been lucky to have had enough money to turn down work I've felt inappropriate. If people want me to do things — if it's for a good cause or for the boys who fought for us — then I try not to let them down.'

Harry died in 1998, but Dame Vera's career continued to go from strength to strength. The year she died she became the oldest singer to get an album into the UK top 40 with her greatest hits collection.

Dame Vera Lynn was born in East Ham, Essex, on 20 March 1917, and she died in Ditchling, Sussex, on 18 June 2020, at the age of 103.

Claudine Mawby

The last of the Mawby Triplets died, aged ninety, at her home in Poole in Dorset. With her sisters, Claudette and Angella, Claudine had made twenty-four films in Hollywood in the Roaring Twenties with the likes of John Barrymore, Gloria Swanson and Mary Pickford. They were the first child stars, and, at the height of their fame, they were honoured by ticker tape parades, had their tiny handprints set in stone at Grauman's Chinese Theatre and served as bridesmaids at the wedding of Joan Crawford and Douglas Fairbanks Jr. The then Prince of Wales — later Edward VIII — fêted them at a garden party at Buckingham Palace and the newspaper magnate William Randolph Hearst and Marion Davies, his mistress, took them to lunch.

The news of Claudine's death made headlines around the world and it hit me hard, not least because she was my mother. Of course, that was how I thought of her: the one person who was always there for me, put up with my screaming as a baby, the usual nonsense during adolescence and became my principal cheerleader after I started work. Until a few weeks of her death, we'd been regularly swimming together in the sea. I think because she'd been educated only on film sets and never worked in an office, she was a uniquely free spirit. She had little, if any, respect for authority and told people exactly what she thought of them. She was an unerringly good judge of character.

It felt strange reading about this film star in the obituaries. She had consigned her extraordinary early life to a few old scrapbooks that I only discovered in her attic after her death. I had an awareness she had acted as a child, but she seldom spoke about it. Once, watching *The Sunshine Boys* — a film about two old Vaudevillians, starring Walter Matthau and George Burns — she casually mentioned that was her in one of the old black and white clips they showed in the opening credits. I think she considered it all to be rather vulgar — and it also brought back an intensely painful memory.

Fame had happened to her accidentally when she arrived in southern California on a liner at the age of four with her parents and two sisters. Her mother Ella had been advised

The Mawby Triplets in costumes designed by Barbara Cartland.
From left to right, Claudette, Angella and Claudine.

by her doctors to take a long break in sunnier climes after an illness. A newspaper photographer had spotted them, and, reckoning three beautiful identical youngsters were something of a novelty, took their picture. It was syndicated across America. Talent scouts from MGM saw it and swiftly signed the girls up to appear in their first film, *The Baby Cyclone*, with Lew Cody.

Others followed in quick succession: *Dance of the Paper Dolls,* one of the earliest colour films, and the original *Broadway Melody*, with Bessie Love, among them. They sang *Singin' in the Rain* with Jack Benny in *The Hollywood Revue of 1929*. My grandparents attempted to explain that they weren't actually triplets: my mother and Claudette were twins, but Angella was eleven months older. The film publicists told them not to fret and billed them as the Mawby Triplets anyway. A cartoon appeared in *Punch* showing the girls on stage with one punter saying to another: 'At least two of them are triplets.'

They were paid an astronomical twenty-five pounds a day and got to meet anyone who was anyone, including George Bernard Shaw. He asked them if they liked acting, and they replied — in unison, according to the *Daily Herald* — 'it's perfectly lovely'. My mother remembered how Shaw had ordered Charlotte, his long-suffering wife, to stay indoors. She'd looked out at them longingly from an upstairs window.

In 1932, after the aviator Charles Lindbergh's twenty-month-old son was kidnapped and murdered, the girls had begun receiving threats, and, on one occasion, a group of men ran their car off the road before being seen off by the burly actor Victor McLaglen, who happened to be travelling with them. The family decided it was time to head home.

The girls appeared in a few films at Elstree after their return, and, in 1936, when they had all reached the age of ten — at the time the minimum age to legally appear on a stage — they starred in the musical *Going Places* at the Savoy Theatre. The outbreak of war put an end to their careers not long afterwards. Infinitely worse, Claudette was killed when one of Hitler's V-1 flying bombs hit a brand new block of flats called Marine Gate where she had been staying in Brighton.

It was, of course, the pain of that which made it so hard for my mother to look at the pictures of three such blissfully happy children in her old scrapbooks. Still, she went on to find another role in life at which she excelled, and that was motherhood. What she understood, above all things, was what mattered in life and what didn't.

Claudine Mawby was born in Hampstead, London, on 10 August 1922, and died in Poole, Dorset, on 13 September 2012.

Barbara Cartland

I took tea with Dame Barbara Cartland at Camfield Place, her vast mansion set in 400 lush acres near Hatfield in Hertfordshire. I was there with about a dozen other journalists to talk to the old girl about her latest romantic novel. It was the occasion that Victoria Coren Mitchell — as she is now known — made me choke on a meringue.

Dame Barbara had asked us all who we thought could play her if a film were ever to be made about her life. One or two obsequious colleagues had suggested Michelle Pfeiffer, certainly for the young Dame Barbara. Another had lamented how sad it was Grace Kelly was no longer alive. Then, in a stage whisper, Victoria suggested, with the proviso that there was a good wig and enough make-up, Robbie Coltrane.

Our hostess was oblivious to the fact that some people found her every utterance, the way she looked and even her very existence, to be inordinately funny. The satirical comedy series *Little Britain* mocked her with a character called Dame Sally Markham — played by Matt Lucas — who reclined on a chaise lounge in a billowing pink dress, dictating romantic drivel, and, eventually getting bored, she told her secretary to make up the words by hoovering up the A–E section of the London telephone directory as nobody would notice.

This lady was, however, a hack just like the rest of us at that tea, albeit a very much wealthier one. She'd started off working as a gossip columnist on the *Daily Express* before starting to produce, like a mother tortoise laying her eggs, some 723 novels. Of course, no one in their right mind would lay any claim to her being a great writer, but she was undoubtedly a great saleswoman. She had made it her business to try to physically embody romance, and, while the end result wasn't everybody's idea of what it was, it was undoubtedly hers and it was clearly all about the colour pink.

Even in later life — and she was into her nineties when we had this tea — her energy was phenomenal. It wasn't just her strict daily writing regime. She also made herself available 24/7 to journalists seeking quotes on just about anything. I had phoned her up once when I had been writing a piece about Ascot, and, of course, she obliged. 'It's quite appalling who they allow into the Royal Enclosure these days. In my day, even individuals who were the innocent parties in divorce cases were generally turned away. I remember how we would look across from the Royal Enclosure at the people opposite and say "Over there, my dear, is the Adulterers' Stand...".'

For a piece on the disgraced Major Ronald Ferguson she was happy, once again, to put in her two-penny worth, saying 'it would really rather be better now if no one mentioned his name'. She was a censorious old thing and whether she was entirely a force for good I am not so sure. She happened to be especially popular in the Middle East and that worried her fellow author, Anthony Burgess. He told me he blamed her for many of the misconceptions about the West in the region and suggested she might even have inadvertently caused wars.

'Anthony is of course talking absolute rot, but I will admit I am not sure it was awfully good for Diana (the late Princess of Wales) to have read my books and nothing else because I don't think they were awfully good for her;

I think they may have given her an idea about love that was not entirely realistic.'

As we got through the meringues and still more cups of Earl Grey in bone china cups, Dame Barbara talked a lot about how appalled she had been that fellow writers, such as Jackie Collins and Judith Krantz, sold their books so overtly on sex. 'I haven't read them, of course, but I am told they are quite disgusting and might more honestly be sold as pornography.'

She'd always felt uneasy about the means the human race set about perpetuating itself. She was said to have broken off her first engagement to a Guards officer when told what sexual intercourse actually involved. She eventually managed to steel herself and had a daughter — Raine Spencer, Countess Spencer (Diana's step-mother) — by her first husband Captain Alexander 'Sachie' George McCorquodale, and two sons, Ian and Glen, by her second husband, Hugh McCorquodale, who was, cosily, her first husband's cousin.

Our conversation moved on to a number of obsessions she had in relation to her health. 'People ask me how I look so good and have so much energy and the answer is royal jelly. Confidentially, I sent a consignment to Margaret Thatcher and she thanked me and said it became a part of her daily diet when she was prime minister.'

She held forth on royal jelly for some time, and, when a journalist from the *Express* attempted to bring the discussion back to sex, she must have misunderstood what he was getting at. I learnt afterwards she had privately sent him a special kind of royal jelly that was, she explained in the accompanying note, efficacious when it came to erectile dysfunction.

Dame Barbara Cartland was born in Birmingham on 9 July 1901, and died in Hertfordshire on 21 May 2000 at the age of ninety-eight.

Fay Wray

The producer told Fay Wray that she was going to have 'the tallest, darkest leading man in Hollywood', and she optimistically thought it might be Cary Grant. It turned out to be a giant ape — or at least an eighteen-inch model of one that was made to look a lot bigger with some technical wizardry — and she was to play his love interest. The film was *King Kong*.

Miss Wray was a feisty eighty-two when I met her as she was promoting her memoirs, which she'd amusingly entitled *On the Other Hand*. There was a picture of her on the cover being held in King Kong's left paw. A part in a classic can weigh heavily on an actor — it's all the fans ever want to talk about for decades and it inevitably results in typecasting — but Miss Wray knew the moment she saw the script that this was the film that was going to make her name.

'The part was going to go to Jean Harlow, but she'd had contractual obligations elsewhere and someone suggested me,' Miss Wray told me, self-deprecatingly. 'I jumped at it because I could see that the script had a marvellous charm about it. It was such a silly story really, but I knew the fellas involved well enough to know they'd make it beautifully and indeed they did. You really can't fault it, even today. The special effects were way ahead of their time, but it isn't even those that make the picture so special. It's the way it makes you care about Kong, so that when eventually he falls to his death from the Empire State Building, it's hard not to shed a tear.'

She had allowed her hair to turn iron grey, but her lipstick was bright red and she had retained a definite twinkle in her eyes. She seemed somewhat startled still to be alive. 'I am about the only person that appears in my book who retains a pulse,' she said. 'I think it will do well, though, as nobody will ever forget the stars of the golden age of Hollywood.'

Still, Miss Wray said making *King Kong* wasn't so glamorous. 'Quite frankly, it was more of an endurance test. The rear-projection process we used making that film — me having to pretend to see the gigantic Kong that would later be added in by the special effects boys — was exhausting. There was one scene that — I kid you not — required me to work for twenty-two hours without a break. It was hard to summon up much energy towards the end when the director shouted "scream, scream for your life, Fay!"'

Other scenes put her in mortal danger. 'The close-ups when I was in Kong's paw were done with the thing attached to a lever that could be raised or lowered, but sometimes the fingers that were supposed to be holding me became loose, and, about forty feet up, I had to shout at the props man when it looked like they were about to snap off and fall to the ground, along with me.'

She felt the film had aged remarkably well and it was worth the effort. 'Sometimes you find yourself making a film where it's really just a job for everyone involved — no one really cares about it — but, with *King Kong*, everyone

Fay Wray with her husband, the screenwriter,
Robert Riskin, in 1942.

involved was a total perfectionist. I think that was really
what made it worth so much more than the sum of its
parts. If any other group of individuals had got together to
make that film, it would almost certainly have descended
into farce. We took it incredibly seriously.'

Miss Wray had never appeared in a real classic before
King Kong, and nor did she after, and, although three-
times married, she joked that the mighty ape was the
most enduring love affair of her life. When, in 2004, Peter
Jackson suggested she appear in a small cameo in his
remake of *King Kong,* she had no hesitation in declining.
'It felt like cheating on my Kong, the only true King,' she
said. When she died later that year at the grand age of
ninety-six, the lights of the Empire State Building —
where she'd played her last big scene with Kong — were
lowered in her honour.

*Fay Wray was born in Alberta, Canada, on 15 September
1907, and died in New York City on 8 August 2004.*

Sylvia Anderson

I f, after more than a half a century, a fictional character is still familiar to generations, the chances are its creator is a star. I would say that about Sylvia Anderson, whom we have to thank for Lady Penelope. 'It was never intended that she would dominate *Thunderbirds* in quite the way she did, and, indeed, she was originally only going to be an occasional walk-on player,' Sylvia told me. 'But she had a quality that just could not be suppressed. Maybe it helped, too, that we made the series at a time when she was allowed to be a terrible snob and wear mink coats and smoke like a chimney, and, of course, all of that differentiated her from other puppets.'

Sylvia didn't exactly play Lady Penelope, but the character was her idea, it was her voice that the viewers heard and the puppet was made very much in her image with exactly the same blonde coiffure. When I met Sylvia at her magnificent home in Bray in Buckinghamshire, she recalled how, when the series started to be aired, there was a kind of movie star glamour to her life.

'In fact, everyone involved in making *Thunderbirds* thought of our little world as Hollywood in microcosm, and so it followed that we thought of our puppets as stars. We actually modelled some of our characters in that, and the other series we created, on real ones. Troy Tempest from *Stingray*, for instance, was based on James Garner and Captain Scarlet on Cary Grant.

'Towards the end, we got a bit carried away and tried to make the perfect composite star — a puppet with Elizabeth Taylor's eyes, Marilyn Monroe's lips and Sophia Loren's nose. Sadly, what we considered to be the perfect face turned out to be a bit bland. We catered for our female audience, too, and tried to make Captain Scarlet overtly sexy. He was the first puppet ever to have five o'clock shadow.'

She said there was a kind of 'madness' about the way they had gone about making *Thunderbirds* with hours, if not sometimes days or even weeks, spent making a particular scene absolutely perfect. Her creative partner was her husband Gerry Anderson. He saw himself very much as an autocratic film-maker of Hollywood's golden age. 'It helped that we had Lew Grade backing us and I wonder now, if we'd tried to do a show like ours — given how obsessional about it we all were — anyone would have given us the time of day.'

Around the time the first feature film version of *Thunderbirds* was released in 1967, it had all started to get too much for her and Gerry and she talked of blazing rows in hotel rooms during a nationwide tour to promote it. 'As a woman producer who was also the creator and voice of the puppet star, I was considered newsworthy. This pleased the publicity department, but not Gerry. In retrospect, I understand better his bruised male ego, but at the time it came as a shock that he came to resent me so bitterly. It had all worked fine between us in the early days, when we were making do in tiny studios and living hand-to-mouth, but, when the money started rolling in, everything changed. Our relationship began as a partnership and a democracy, but ended up a dictatorship.'

Their marriage and professional partnership finally came to a bitter end in 1975, and Gerry — in what Sylvia described as 'an act of madness' — sold the rights to *Thunderbirds* so they never made a penny out of the constant re-runs, video and merchandise sales, which she said were worth untold millions.

She had, however, got custody of their son, Gerry Jnr, (taking his mother's side, he decided to go by the name of Andy) and the puppets. In 1995 when I interviewed her, she was about to sell the latter off. Flatteringly for her, the auctioneers Phillips put the highest price — £25,000 — on Lady Penelope. 'We've been through a lot together, but she was starting to depress me,' Sylvia said of her decision to let her go. 'I look older each year, but she just stays the same, damn her. It's like *The Picture of Dorian Gray* in reverse!'

Sylvia Anderson was born in Camberwell, London, on 25 March 1927, and died in Bray on 15 March 2016, at the age of eighty-eight.

Sylvia and Gerry Anderson on the set of *Thunderbirds*.

Marcel Marceau

Of all the people in all the world, mime artists must seem like the least promising subjects for an interview. Marcel Marceau was, however, a joy to talk to. And to behold.

It was the summer of 1990 and the scene was the restaurant at the Ritz in London, where the head waiter was clearly no respecter of stars. Marceau didn't have a tie and the dress code was the dress code. 'I think I have the solution,' he said, after pondering the problem. 'I shall mime a tie.'

The head waiter was not amused, and Marceau, looking a bit like the dejected clown he so often portrayed on stage, retreated to his suite and returned with a physical tie. I observed how he walked and moved his hands and was struck how, even in conversation, every movement was perfectly judged. He seemed to have got so used to communicating with his entire body that it had become second nature to him.

'You must know that I am slightly deaf,' he informed me, unpromisingly, after the waiter had taken our orders. 'It's likely that you will ask me a lot of questions that I will be unable to hear.' The deafness turned out to be selective. Questions about his one-man show at Sadler's Wells in London, whispered even, got through immediately. Questions about his private life, shouted even, drew a blank time after time.

Marceau was on his third marriage and fourth child by the time we met, but it was his courage during the war that interested me more. As a Jewish youngster, on the run

132

in occupied France, he had worked with the Resistance and was credited with helping innumerable children flee the Nazis. His fluency in English and German eventually landed him a job as a liaison officer with George Patton's Third Army

I persisted and spoke ever louder, but he eventually said to me very quietly: 'It was all a very long time ago and I did what anyone who loves life and his fellow human beings would have done, and, seriously, a lot of people risked a lot more — and achieved much greater things — than I did during that time of madness.'

Marceau saw mime as a natural extension of acting after he'd trained at the Charles Dullin School of Dramatic Art, in Paris. 'Mime is truth,' he said. 'Words are fundamentally untrustworthy. Just look at the kind of people that use words the most — politicians, journalists...' He grinned, impishly.

Marceau was then sixty-seven and had come to have a pretty realistic opinion of members of my trade. He had been mercilessly lampooned in a lot of newspaper interviews. Rowan Atkinson had also had a go at mime artists in a sketch in the satirical television series *Not the Nine O'Clock News.* 'Mime is my life so of course I take it seriously,' Marceau said. 'I may be a wealthy man now, but I did not ever expect to be one when I began forty years ago. It looked then as if I would be going against the tide all my life. Nobody can doubt my commitment.'

Marceau took no wine with his lunch and told me he exercised every day. He looked good for his age. 'It is my work that keeps me young,' he said. 'For me, it is the elixir of youth.' He had in the past been more concerned about the longevity of mime as an art form. He'd gone on record as saying that while opera would survive the death of any opera singer — no matter how illustrious — he wasn't sure if mime wouldn't eventually be buried with him.

The eponymous school of mime he founded in Paris had, however, given him grounds for hope. 'There are some very talented mime artists around,' he said. 'Mime is too great an art to die.'

Marcel Marceau was born in Strasbourg, France, on 22 March 1923, and died in Cahors, France, on 22 September 2007, aged eighty-four.

Maggie Smith

When I went to see Dame Maggie Smith appearing in *A German Life* at the Bridge Theatre in London in 2019, I was invited backstage to see her after the curtain went down. The octogenarian actress had been performing alone for one hour and forty minutes, playing Brunhilde Pomsel, Joseph Goebbels' secretary, talking with chilling insouciance about what she had seen and heard during the war years in Berlin. It had been an emotionally and physically draining performance, and, towards the end of the run, Maggie had every right to head home immediately it was over to get some sleep.

There she was, however, in her dressing room, poised, alert and holding court to a group of admirers and friends, including the actress Frances Barber, and coming out with one-liners worthy of Violet Crawley, the Dowager Countess of Grantham, in the hit television series *Downton Abbey.* Frances had asked her if she planned to attend Sir Ian McKellen's forthcoming eightieth birthday party and she said she'd love to, paused for a moment, and then inquired as to the venue. Frances told her it was going to be in Bolton. 'Bolton?' riposted Maggie, in a voice that cracked us all up because, in its affected sense of shock, it was pure Violet Crawley.

There are two sides to this actress, which goes some way towards explaining why she is so entertaining: the professional in her, who is congenitally incapable of saying no to good offers of work, and then the private, grounded Maggie, who just wants to be left alone to potter about her garden in the Sussex countryside. 'I sighed when I read the script to *A German Life* because it was something different for me and I knew I had to do it, but I also knew how exhausting it was going to be,' she told us. 'Takes total concentration, night after night, to get into the head of someone like Brunhilde. I can't see why I can't just accept quick cameo parts in films, like others who've reached my age do, and be in and out and back watering the roses in the afternoon.'

The private Maggie had regularly implored the *Downton Abbey* writer Julian Fellowes to do away with her character in his long-running series. 'Every time I see a *Downton* script, I always look hopefully for my death scene,' she told us. 'Always I am disappointed.' Of course, Julian appreciated that Maggie was an indispensable part of the Downton fixtures and fittings, and, indeed, she invests every project she involves herself in with that indefinable quality called class.

On screen and on stage, Maggie has always made it look deceptively easy. I remember her brilliant performances in plays such as *Lettice and Lovage*, alongside Margaret Tyzack, and her magnificent Lady Bracknell in *The Importance of Being Earnest*, as well as the early film appearances that really made her name internationally, such as the title role in *The Prime of Miss Jean Brodie*, and, later, as an Oscar nominee in Neil Simon's *California Suite*, which, ironically, won her a real-life Oscar.

Talking with her old friends Eileen Atkins, Judi Dench and Joan Plowright in Roger Mitchell's documentary *Nothing Like a Dame*, it was clear that Maggie had, in common with the other great actresses, to cope with her share of despair. After her second husband, the playwright Beverley Cross, died in 1998, she poignantly admitted: 'It seems a bit pointless, going on, on one's own, and not having someone to share it with.'

Maggie Smith in the BBC's *The Millionairess* (1972).

She has had a series of battles, too, with her health over the years, and when, in 2007, I had the unenviable task of calling her agent to inquire if it was true that she had been diagnosed with breast cancer, no attempt was made to deny it or to ask for privacy. Maggie, like her old friend Lord Olivier before her, did not wish to stigmatise cancer: she had it, she fought it and she saw it off, and that was all there was to it. I think she is so funny on and off stage because ultimately she understands how cruel life can be, and she knows that, if only for a few moments, making people laugh spares them that reality.

Dame Maggie Smith was born in Ilford, Essex, on 28 December 1934.

Maggie Smith played Desdemona to Laurence Olivier's Othello at the National Theatre in 1964.

Toby Stephens

Toby Stephens' wife, Anna-Louise, had lately presented him with an 8lb 4oz baby girl, whom they had decided to name Tallulah. When Toby informed his mother, Dame Maggie Smith, she took a sharp intake of breath. 'She thought of Tallulah Bankhead, a Hollywood actress of some repute,' he said. 'She told me "I love the name, of course, but you must understand that she was a very naughty woman. She was addicted to cocaine, and had, among other things, a huge lesbian following".'

His mother delivered the lines with her customary aplomb, but then she can't help being — as Toby's father, Sir Robert Stephens, once was — innately theatrical. Conspicuous parents can be a huge burden upon their children, and, for a time, Toby admitted the endless questions he used to get asked about the pair, who starred together in the 1969 film *The Prime of Miss Jean Brodie,* were a source of irritation. 'Now it makes me rather proud and I sort of understand the fascination,' he said. 'If you've parents like mine, it's important to try to learn what you can from them, but then make your own way.'

The year was 2014 and Toby was about to appear in a production of *A Doll's House* at the Donmar. In a coffee bar nearby, he seemed to be going out of his way to be as untheatrical as possible. He certainly had no interest in trying to recreate, with his actress wife, the glamorous life Maggie and Robert had once lived. He was acutely aware that an ability to act was not necessarily his only birthright.

Around the turn of the millennium, he realised his father's alcoholism had been passed down to him too, and, since it was beginning to take its toll on his work, he resolved never to drink again. Sir Robert had died at the age of sixty-four, in 1995, after liver and kidney transplants, but Toby said he would have been furious if anyone had ever suggested to him that he was addicted to booze.

'Of course, he was an alcoholic in the same way that I am, in that he had no control over his drinking. If I were to have one drink now, I would want another and it would be agony if I couldn't. I simply decided to spare myself that by not allowing myself the first glass. People go on about my father's demons being handed on to me, but I think, where the booze is concerned, it is actually a boring biochemical thing that has been passed on to me. I associate my alcoholism with diabetes, as both Robert and his sister had that disease. I have a friend who has been through the same thing. A lot of alcoholics who give up drinking then become addicted to cakes, chocolate, dessert. I really do believe it stems from the same imbalance within us.'

He reckoned it's low self-esteem that drives a lot of people into acting, the chance to seek refuge in other characters and then there's 'the wonderful quick fix of applause'. That need for validation was almost certainly a factor in his father's addiction, too, to sex. Toby and Anna-Louise — who he first met at the acting school LAMDA — have, however, managed to live together contentedly. He said that had proved possible for him only because of the benign influence of his mother, who managed, with her second husband Beverley Cross, to give him and his brother Christopher (also an actor, with the stage name Chris Larkin) a perfectly tranquil upbringing in rural Sussex.

Tellingly, it was Cross that Toby referred to as his father, and his natural father he referred to simply as Robert.

'Dad was a calming influence on all of us. My mother found the break-up of her marriage to Robert very painful because she still loved him very much, but his drinking and all the other issues had made her position untenable. God knows what kind of an upbringing I would have had if my mother's relationship with Robert hadn't broken up when it did, but I think it was good for me and my brother that things worked out the way that they did.'

He seemed at ease with himself in both his personal and professional life. When I inquired about the rumours he might one day take over from Daniel Craig as James Bond, he laughed. 'God knows, I could use the money, but it won't happen. They had enough problems with a blond

Bond. The idea of someone with reddish hair getting the part would cause insurrection.'

His one brush with Bond — as the villain in *Die Another Day* with Pierce Brosnan — was, he felt, an aberration. 'I have no idea how I got the part. I remember meeting Lee Tamahori, the director, and asking him about my character, as they had only sent me three pages of script. He said, "Well, in a nutshell, you are playing a Korean who has been genetically modified into being a westerner," and I must say he lost me somewhere in that sentence. I had a lot of fun making that film, but honestly it wasn't where I came from or what I was a part of, and I subsequently just got on with what I had been doing before.'

Toby Stephens was born in London on 21 April 1969.

Toby Stephens appeared with Aamir Kahn in *The Rising* (2005).

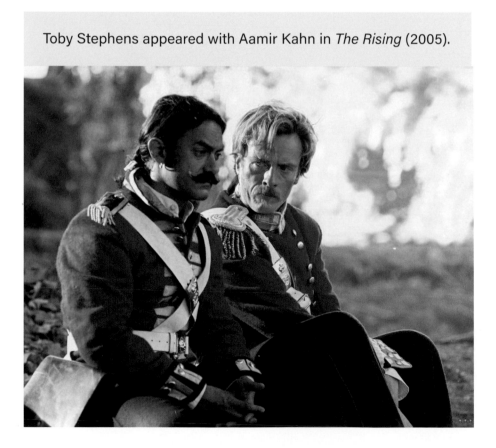

Diana Rigg

I t was at the Chichester Festival that I last saw Dame
Diana Rigg. Not on stage, but sitting directly in front
of me as her daughter, Rachael Stirling, starred in
a revival of Sir David Hare's play *Plenty*. She glowed
with maternal pride.

The fine actress's death, not long afterwards, at the age
of eighty-two, came as a shock. She'd been diagnosed
with untreatable cancer, but told only those closest to
her. She had trodden the boards herself only recently in
My Fair Lady on Broadway. She appeared, too, in *Game
of Thrones*. That television series brought her awards and
great reviews, but, not remotely vain, she admitted she'd
never troubled to watch it.

I first met her in the late 1990s at a classy hotel in
Holland Park in west London. Her faith in members of my
trade had, at that point, been all but exhausted. 'I mean
I've done my time as a serious actress, but it's always
the men I've slept with or *The Avengers* or James Bond
you people ever want to talk about,' she said. I asked her
why she'd refused to talk to a woman journalist from my
paper. 'Women journalists are always the same. They
come along, establish a sense of sisterhood, make me feel
I can trust them, and then, every time, they betray it.
Never again.'

There was an unworldliness to her — even an innocence
— that meant she could never understand why she made
such great copy. In the 1960s, she lived for eight years
with the director Philip Saville, and made it clear she had

no interest in marrying her older and already-spoken-for lover. 'Respectability,' she said, 'is so terribly boring.'

She went on to marry Menachem Gueffen, an Israeli painter, in 1973, and, after their divorce in 1976, began a relationship with Archie Stirling, a theatrical producer and former officer in the Scots Guards, and provided him with a daughter, Rachael. Rigg and Stirling married five years after the birth. She divorced Stirling in 1990 after his affair with the actress Joely Richardson.

In some snobby quarters, Rigg was regarded as not being in quite the same league as fellow dames, such as Maggie Smith and Judi Dench. She had, however, played a wide range of roles for the Royal Shakespeare Company with distinction in the 1960s — but, fairly or unfairly, came to be defined by her performance as Emma Peel in *The Avengers*. A lot of folk couldn't quite accept that a woman could at one and the same time be a serious actress, but also unbelievably sexy, make popular films and television shows and enjoy the company of a succession of men who happened to interest her.

Of the James Bond film *On Her Majesty's Secret Service*, she said she 'had a ball'. So far from feuding with its star George Lazenby — as the tabloids made out — she insisted she was actually quite 'motherly' to him as she could see how he couldn't quite handle the position he'd found himself in. Lazenby confirmed this in an interview after Rigg's death: she gave him practical advice and tried to help.

In her work, as with her private life, the one question Rigg asked herself before consenting was whether it would be any fun or not. That led to her accepting a part in the camp 1973 horror film *Theatre of Blood,* when she was Vincent Price's leading lady. 'The moment they told me it was about an actor killing off theatre critics, I was there,' she laughed. 'I could just tell what fun it'd be to work with Vinnie and I wasn't disappointed.'

Rigg could sense that the actor was bored and played Cupid between him and Coral Browne, another of the

Diana Rigg co-starred with Patrick Macnee in *The Avengers*.

stars in the film. 'I had them both round to dinner and the rapport was immediate. They were two of the brightest and funniest people in the world. It seemed to me inevitable they'd hit it off.' Rigg's instinct proved to be quite right and the pair ended up marrying the following year. 'I had no idea that Vinnie was married at the time I introduced him to Coral, but I've no regrets. It all worked out very well.'

All Rigg wanted was to be happy, and she wanted the people around her to be happy, too. 'I leave judgement to others,' she said. 'I haven't the time to dispense that.'

Dame Diana Rigg was born in Doncaster, Yorkshire, on 20 July 1938, and died in London on 10 September 2020, aged eighty-two.

Angela Lansbury

I've seen a few actors treading the boards in advanced old age. Rex Harrison in *The Admirable Crichton* a few years before his death, when one of the critics noted that he had 'no more than a nodding acquaintance with the script'. Laurence Olivier played a space age god more adroitly in the Cliff Richard rock musical *Time,* but the rigours of a long run were not for him and he dispatched a three-dimensional hologram of himself to do the heavy-lifting. Then there was Dame Angela Lansbury who, in her eighty-ninth year, portrayed Madame Arcati — in the flesh and word-perfect — in *Blithe Spirit* in the West End.

I'd seen Michael Blakemore's production first on Broadway four years previously and had been astonished then that Lansbury could summon the energy to play the eccentric medium and clairvoyant. The little dance routine that she did to conjure up the ghost of Elvira was perhaps marginally more restrained in the later production, but the voice was still strong, she stood tall and without a stick, she was fully cognisant of her marks and she looked and acted like a lady who was no more than half her age. Above all things, it was clear that her star quality hadn't faded at all.

There was a line in Noël Coward's play in which Madame Arcati, taking umbrage at complaints about her handiwork, riposted: 'I am a professional.' That, of course, is what the actress has always been in a career that has spanned almost eight decades. Rupert Everett, who co-

starred in the Broadway production of *Blithe Spirit,* used the word 'correct' to describe her. As her leading man, he added that he was expected to lunch with her once a week to discuss the production and ways in which it could be improved. She told him every production, no matter what it was, could always be improved.

In her dressing room at the Gielgud Theatre, there was an air of order that radiated around Lansbury, with her costumes neatly laid out, her make-up in serried rows, and every syllable she uttered chosen with care and enunciated with precision. She was used to questions about retirement, and whether she ever got tired, but she was simply not willing to indulge them. More than that, she considered them to be ageist. 'I plan to take a short break at my home in Ireland when the show closes, but I see no point in retirement as I am an actress and acting is my life,' she said, briskly. 'I've ambitions still that I would like to realise. I rather like the idea of doing Enid Bagnold's *The Chalk Garden,* as a matter of fact. Now that is an interesting play. I also rather fancy the idea of a Restoration comedy.'

Still, she was aware that it was her age that made people marvel at her and it was almost certainly part of what motivated the standing ovations she received nightly. 'I accept in some quarters there is astonishment that I am still able to put one leg in front of the other,' she said with a smile. 'Older characters should, however, be played by older actors. It pleases me that I'm not the only person in my eighties now appearing in the West End with Robert Vaughn doing so well in *Twelve Angry Men*.'

Remarkably, audiences were applauding her not just at the end of the show, but also when she made her first entrance. I mentioned that the last actor I had seen accorded that honour was the arch Republican Charlton Heston in *The Caine Mutiny Court-Martial*. 'I'd really rather you hadn't told me that as it puts it into perspective,' the lifelong Democrat replied. 'Charlton Heston, well, goodness me.'

Lansbury said one of the joys of a career as long as hers was being able to connect with different generations in different ways. I told her I'd always associate her with the film *Bedknobs and Broomsticks*, which I saw as a child. 'Maybe in terms of my film work, it's *Gaslight* for the generation before yours, and I suppose *Murder, She Wrote* for the young-uns.

'I am lucky to have survived in the business for as long as I have. I sometimes think I was fortunate not to have been especially beautiful when I was young. It makes it easier to make the transition into middle age. Casting directors can't seem to forgive beautiful young people for getting older and less beautiful. The other thing, I suppose, that's important is to always try to be polite, no matter what. That helps a great deal as people won't mind working with you again.'

Dame Angela Lansbury was born in London on 16 October 1925.

Eileen Atkins

My mother looked at me as if she'd hatched a snake, but then I could be vile to her and to my family,' said Dame Eileen Atkins. 'My parents were angry people, frustrated with their lot in life, and I inherited their anger. I've always put my career before everyone and I've been very selfish. I think it's a good thing I never had any children as I would almost certainly have passed on my anger to them. I'd have been a terrible mother.'

It's as well that Atkins never got to write pieces about herself as she was a much kinder and gentler person than she liked to let on. I first met her in 2007 at the restaurant at the Almeida theatre in north London, when she was about to open in Frank McGuinness's *There Came a Gypsy Riding*. She seemed at pains to make the point that she was the bit of 'rough' compared to, say, Dame Judi Dench and Dame Maggie Smith. 'Of course, I'm not as polished, and nor do I have their confidence, but then I'm the one that came from a council estate,' she said. 'That makes me very different from them in a way that's quite fundamental.'

Although she'd had some big television hits — *The Crown, Doc Martin, Cranford* and she was the co-creator of *Upstairs, Downstairs* — it was true, perhaps, that she was the least famous of the dames, but that was, to be fair, a calculated decision on her part. She felt stardom could be an encumbrance for a serious actor who wanted to 'disappear into a part'. 'Take my role in the film

adaptation of Ronnie Harwood's play *The Dresser*, where I was playing the dowdy manager of a small repertory company. If I'd been a star, I just don't think I could have pulled that off. Everybody would be going "look at that big star playing that dowdy woman". The part required me to blend into the background and I even chose clothes that would help me to do that. It was necessary then not to be noticed.'

Atkins was a woman of fierce loyalties. She and Harwood went back years and that film was a reunion for the two of them and Albert Finney — who played the domineering 'Sir' — as he had trained as an actor with Harwood at the Royal Academy of Dramatic Art. It was striking how all of Atkins' friends were protective of her, but maybe there was an awareness among them that ultimately all Atkins needed protection from is herself.

She was always recklessly, dangerously honest and that's what made her such compelling company. She talked to me about her 'big mouth' almost as if it was an external entity, quite beyond her control. One could but recall the fuss when she let slip to a journalist that *The Batman* heart-throb Colin Farrell — forty-two years her junior — had made a pass at her. She didn't, of course, mean to embarrass Farrell — and he took it very well and even came to see her in a play in New York just after the story broke — and, until she saw the headlines, she hadn't imagined anyone would have been interested. 'Colin may have thought he wanted me, but I recognised my allure lay in his mind rather than my body and the relationship was never consummated,' she insisted. They remained friends and I could see why, as Atkins has acquired extraordinary wisdom over the course of a life that began in poverty in east London. She had gone on to battle cancer and her private life has been eventful and often painful.

Certainly, she had come to understand the preposterousness of sex and told me that 'infidelity is one of the last things you should fall out with someone over'. Her first husband — whom she married at twenty-two — was the actor Julian Glover, but he had an affair with Sarah Miles and they divorced. It's characteristic of Atkins that she remained friends with both Glover and Miles. She also owned up to a long-running affair herself with 'a well-known American who is now dead,' but whom she never named, lest it upset his widow. There was also a dalliance with Edward Fox, but, as much as she loved him, it ended after an ultimatum. 'A job came up for me in America and he said to me that if I took it then we would be finished,' she said. 'I took it and we finished.'

She went on to have a long and happy marriage with the advertising director Bill Shepherd, but she accepted that her career had always been her first love. She had been taking Mogadon to get to sleep for the past forty-four years — lately doubling the dose — but she looked a remarkably youthful seventy-two when we'd first met, with luminous pale blue eyes, regally high cheekbones and glossy, auburn hair. There was a time in more recent years when I was going to write her authorised biography, but we eventually agreed that it was a terrible idea. She knew she wouldn't be able to help herself and I'd have felt guilt about monetising her compulsive indiscretion. It would, however, have been one hell of a book.

Dame Eileen Atkins was born in Lower Clapton, London, on 16 June 1934.

Eileen Atkins and Sian Philips at the Royal Academy of Arts.

Ronald Harwood

I t fascinated Sir Ronald Harwood how individuals responded to stark moral dilemmas. He never, however, judged, and preferred to etch out his characters in shades of grey — rather than blacks and whites — and that's what made his plays and screenplays so intriguing.

Hitler's favourite conductor, Wilhelm Furtwängler, in Harwood's *Taking Sides,* is thus no cartoon baddie, any more than the composer Richard Strauss, who stood by his Jewish librettist, Stefan Zweig, in Nazi Germany in *Collaboration,* is a boring saint. 'I leave it to audiences to judge as I don't feel equipped as I've never had to face such choices,' Harwood told me. 'I've no idea what I would have done in their shoes at a time like that.'

Harwood and I had first come face-to-face as we were waiting for our coats after the party to mark the opening of the Saatchi Gallery in the old County Hall building in London. Two disgruntled lines of guests had converged and he thought I was queue-barging and I thought he was. It could have gone either way: either a row or the start of a friendship. Happily, we got talking.

He's probably best known for his play *The Dresser,* which became a successful film starring Albert Finney, Tom Courtenay and Eileen Atkins, and, more recently, a less successful television drama starring Ian McKellen and Anthony Hopkins. Harwood picked up an Oscar, too, for *The Pianist,* and had big hits with *Quartet* — a play, then a film — and *Cry, the Beloved Country.*

He started out as an actor and trained at the Royal Academy of Dramatic Art alongside Finney, Peter O'Toole and Alan Bates. There was a period working as the dresser to the actor-manager Donald Wolfit — that was what inspired the play of that name — but probably the high point of his early career was playing a PC Gale in a long-forgotten television series called *Formula for Danger*.

He recognised he didn't have what it took to make it in acting and switched to writing. He was a regular scripting the television series *Tales of the Unexpected* — no easy task, as he felt Roald Dahl had 'little gift for characterisation' — but there were times when money was scarce. Once he even considered working on a building site. He never wanted anything but the best for his wife Natasha, a descendant of Russian nobility, and their three children, and just kept banging away at his typewriter.

Material success, his Oscar and a knighthood came to him late in life, and certainly at a point when they couldn't change him. It was typical of him that he told a Tory politician at his club on one of his final visits that

he considered Brexit to be 'a load of bollocks'. He hated, above all things, hypocrisy.

I was passing by his flat in Chelsea between the lockdowns and phoned on his mobile to suggest a cup of tea and that was when he told me his family had 'forcibly evacuated' him to the relative safety of Sussex. 'I miss my friends, my club, the theatre, your terrible reviews and my children without their bloody masks on,' he grumbled. He died not long afterwards at the age of eighty-five.

Sir Ronald Harwood was born in Cape Town, South Africa, on 9 November 1934 and died in Chichester, Sussex, on 8 September 2020.

John Mortimer

Sir John Mortimer once gave me some advice. 'If you find a vulgar bone in your body,' he said, 'treasure it, nurture it, exercise it, make it as strong as you possibly can and it'll end up making you very rich indeed.' Mortimer was a highly intelligent man whose life arguably amounted to a celebration of those words. Pot-bellied, bespectacled and with a rather absurd comb-over, he showed, too, that charm often more than made up for conventional good looks so far as the opposite sex was concerned.

I was a member of the same London club as he was and saw him there and at literary lunches and parties and he rather touchingly took an interest in my career. 'Don't write clever-clever stuff,' he told me, when I mentioned I had aspirations to be a playwright, 'write something that people will actually want to watch.' Mortimer monetised just about every experience he had in life by turning it into a drama of some kind. As anyone who has seen his play *A Voyage Round My Father* will know, it was his father — a barrister played in the television version by Laurence Olivier — who wanted him to follow him into the legal profession.

Mortimer was called to the bar at twenty-five, took silk when he was forty-three, and appeared in a number of high profile cases, which often turned on the issue of freedom of expression. He also enjoyed defending murderers, certainly more than individuals in divorce cases. 'I much preferred murderers because, having

eliminated the one person who bugged them in their lives, they tended to have found a certain peace. People who were getting divorced were still, of course, full of rage and I found them rather trying.'

He had originally wanted to be an actor and admitted his heart was never really in the law. He was also invariably tired by the time he got to court as it was his habit to get up first thing each day to indulge his real passion — writing plays, screenplays and books. Still, his time in courtrooms proved useful source material for *Rumpole of the Bailey,* which began life as a BBC *Play for Today* and later became a long-running ITV series with Leo McKern in the title role. Frustrated actor that he always was, Mortimer couldn't resist periodically appearing in cameo roles.

His television adaptation of Evelyn Waugh's *Brideshead Revisited* almost certainly represented the apogee of his writing career: a hugely commercial, but also — while he'd be loath to admit it — cerebral triumph. He told me how he had gone to Castle Howard in Yorkshire to see some scenes being filmed — 'one of the biggest thrills of my life' — and to dine with Olivier, who played Lord Marchmain. Mortimer idolised the great actor and had written for him not just in *A Voyage Round My Father,* but also *The Ebony Tower* and the Otto Preminger thriller *Bunny Lake is Missing.*

Mortimer, however, loved all actors — sometimes, perhaps, a little too much. In 2004, I heard he'd had a surfeit of port one evening and blurted out at a dinner party that he had a so-far-publicly-unacknowledged child by Wendy Craig, an actress who, thanks to television series such as *Butterflies* and *Not in Front of the Children,* seemed to epitomise family values. I nervously broached this with Mortimer, and, to my astonishment, he confirmed it immediately and I knew I had a front page story. Craig had got to know Mortimer when she had appeared in his first full-length West End play, *The Wrong Side of the Park,* in 1960. Their son, who was named Ross, was raised by Craig and her husband, Jack Bentley, the show business writer and musician, whose name he took.

Ross, too, was willing to talk about the great family secret, relieved in a way to be finally unburdened of it. Craig saw, however, dignity in silence. 'I just don't see that it is anyone's business and I don't understand why John has suddenly felt the need to tell the world,' she said. Old men like, of course, to boast of their sexual conquests, and women are, by and large, a lot less vulgar.

Sir John Mortimer was born in Hampstead on 21 April 1923, and died in Turville Heath, Buckinghamshire, on 16 January 2009, aged eighty-five.

Peter Bowles

It was the word 'luvvies' that introduced me to Peter Bowles. I'd used it in the way journalists generally do as a light-hearted, if lazy and clichéd, way of describing actors and it had provoked a debate in the letters column of *The Stage,* the newspaper of the theatrical profession. It was agreed by the likes of David Suchet and Marc Sinden that the term was offensive.

I hadn't, of course, meant it to be and was all set to write a piece apologising when Bowles telephoned. 'It so happens it was an actor who coined the term "luvvie," so I can't see how actors can really make a fuss about it,' he said. He maintained it was his old friend James Villiers — an aristocratic actor best known for films such as *The Nanny, Joseph Andrews* and *For Your Eyes Only* — who'd first used it as a term of endearment for colleagues and it had somehow stuck.

Bowles was, in his day, one of the best-known actors in the country, with roles in hugely popular television series such as *Rumpole of the Bailey, Only When I Laugh, The Bounder, The Irish R.M.* and, of course, *To the Manor Born* — in which he appeared as a nouveau riche tycoon, allegedly based on the late Sir James Goldsmith. He'd also played a gossip columnist in a series he'd himself created called *Lytton's Diary.* It was based very obviously on my old boss Nigel Dempster of the *Daily Mail.*

Bowles had caught Dempster very well — a complicated mixture of old-school charm, irascibility and an ever-so-subtle campness — and the two had become great friends.

As a stunt to promote the series, Bowles had come into the *Mail* office to take charge of Dempster's column for a day. The sub-editor who'd worked with him had told me it was 'hellish' because Bowles and Dempster had gone out for a very long lunch and wine was taken. The actor, when he got back, couldn't countenance writing anything unpleasant about any of his friends. The problem was he had so many friends it got perilously close to deadline with the page still entirely blank.

I suggested to Bowles that we meet for lunch at Le Caprice, and, to my delight, he accepted. This was not long after he'd turned seventy, but he'd hardly changed at all since his glory days on television when twenty million viewers would tune in regularly to see him sparring with Penelope Keith in *To the Manor Born.* He was unassuming, modest and emotionally literate. He was also immaculately dressed in a three-piece suit. Dempster had died a few years earlier and we remembered the old monster fondly. We recalled how, when one of Dempster's staff had complained that he'd thrown a copy of *Who's Who* at her, he'd laconically told an industrial tribunal that she'd 'at least been hit by all the right people'.

Of Villiers, Bowles also had affectionate memories. He was a heroic drinker and had managed to keep pace with Peter O'Toole, and, even more dauntingly, the old character actor Ronald Fraser. Bowles said he always thought it sad Villiers hadn't been allowed to reprise the role of Lord Thurlow in the screen version of *The Madness of George III* after he'd made such a fine job of creating the part on stage. One of the locations for the film version was Arundel in Sussex, where Villiers lived, and it had been painful for the old actor to turn a corner one day and see John Wood playing the role he'd set his heart on reprising.

Bowles had had moments of despair in his own career and made bad decisions as well as good ones — he turned down the part of Tom in *The Good Life* — but, in recent years, he's arguably turned in some of the finest performances of his career, notably as an old gent who found love in a nursing home in the film *Lilting*, and, a few years later, as Sylvia Syms' husband in *Together*. I dropped him a line to say how great he'd been and the reply was typically grounded. Bowles knew what mattered in life — Susan, his wife of more than sixty years, and their children, perhaps most of all — and, as for career triumphs and disasters, he'd learnt to treat those two impostors just the same.

Peter Bowles was born in London on 16 October 1936.

Ian Lavender

apt Mainwaring and his magnificent men in *Dad's Army* transcend politics, class and even time. I got to meet Ian Lavender, who played Private Pike, when he was seventy-five, and one of the last surviving members of that flawless cast. He gave me an intriguing insight into the way the scriptwriters Jimmy Perry and David Croft had created the characters. 'In a way, we weren't acting,' Lavender admitted. 'If you look at the earliest episodes, you'll see they are very different to the ones that followed. The reason was that Jimmy and David had got to know all of the actors and they started to write the scripts around our personalities.'

So was the young Lavender really as dim as Pike? 'I would say we were both naive. *Dad's Army* was virtually my first job out of drama school and I hardly knew one end of a TV camera from the other. The "stupid boy" tag was never in the script. Arthur Lowe — playing Capt Mainwaring — once said it to me during rehearsals and it stuck. The facial tic the writers gave me in one episode came from something they'd seen me doing between takes. Even the long scarf I wore was mine, but I didn't wear it because my mother was worried about my croup, but because I was doing a play at the time we started making the series and I needed to disguise the long hair the part required.'

The uneasy relationship between Capt Mainwaring and Sgt Wilson was also inspired by how Lowe and John Le Mesurier — the actors playing the respective parts — treated each other. Lowe was resentful that Le Mesurier

was paid more than he was. 'Arthur was pompous and John a bit vague, but a bit of an old charmer who had an eye for the ladies and liked a drink,' said Lavender. 'Arthur saw himself as the senior man on the set, as he was in the platoon.'

The other characters were also made-to-measure for the actors. John Laurie, who played Fraser, could be cantankerous, and, after playing just about every major role in Shakespeare, would say to Lavender how he regarded the series as infra dig. Clive Dunn, whose catch-phrase as Corporal Jones was 'don't panic', was indeed prone to panic; Frank Williams, who played the Vicar, a bit fey; and Joe Beck, who played Walker, really was a bit of a spiv, and so it went on.

For all that, the motley group made a great ensemble. 'I think it was the fact we were all really theatre people,' said Lavender. 'Knowing your lines, being on the set at the right time and doing the best you could were all real marks of pride. I don't remember anybody ever calling in sick, which was an achievement for quite such an elderly cast.'

Lavender couldn't ever see *Dad's Army* disappearing from the television schedules and believed it had given the cast members a kind of immortality. Certainly, his own fans will never allow him to grow old. 'When they write in, asking me to send them a signed photograph, they never seem to understand who the old guy is if I send them an up-to-date one,' he said. 'So now I just send them the ancient ones of me in the show and that seems to placate them.'

Ian Lavender was born in Birmingham on 16 February 1946.

Simon Callow

Simon Callow has a splendidly dramatic face, a splendidly dramatic bearing and a splendidly dramatic voice. A more splendidly dramatic man it is hard to imagine.

He was directing *Carmen Jones* at the Old Vic when I met him in 1991 and he chose a splendidly dramatic spot for us to do the interview: on two chairs on the deserted stage. I realised, looking out at the vast auditorium, that the view from where we were sitting was every bit, if not more, impressive than the view from the stalls. 'Well, that is what it is to be an actor,' said Callow, mellifluously. 'And, of course, it can become an addiction.'

The chance to direct, rather than act, in the musical created by Georges Bizet and Oscar Hammerstein II was, however, too good a chance for Callow to miss and the one word that kept recurring in the reviews was 'energetic'. 'I was a hyperactive child and I've since felt compelled to put great energy into just about every job I've ever held,' he said. 'I do think though that you should always give everything you've got, no matter what the job is, otherwise there really is not point to it.'

He was then forty-one and up for new challenges, no matter what they were. 'If someone came along and asked me to be the next Dalai Lama, I'd probably agree. I suppose I can't stand the idea of turning down a job that sounds exciting and then wondering what would have happened if I'd taken it.' Callow was a bundle of nervous energy on that stage, his hands in constant motion to illuminate what he was saying and he'd occasionally jump off his chair and continue the conversation walking around me. He simply couldn't sit still. He admitted he'd not actually cared for *Carmen Jones* when he'd first seen it. 'It seemed like wall-to-wall monosodium glutamate, but I've since discovered that there was actually very little wrong with the raw material, only the interpretations.'

Callow had impressed Ismail Merchant so much when he'd appeared in his film *A Room with a View*, in the preceding decade, that he'd asked him to direct *The Ballad of the Sad Café*, which told the unlikely story of a woman who fell in love with a hunchbacked dwarf who, in turn, ended up falling in love with the woman's husband. 'When it was premièred at the Berlin Film Festival a lot of people clapped, but there were some others that booed. It's the boos that I remember.'

Like Toad of Toad Hall, Callow's enthusiasms could be transient. He got bored of appearing on stage in Alan Bennett's *Single Spies* long before its West End run finished, and, so far as *Carmen Jones* was concerned, he intended to leave it in the hands of an assistant director once it was up and running. 'Don't get the impression that I move effortlessly from one job to another. Sadly, I'm not one of the chosen few who can do no wrong. I have to work very hard. I have to keep proving myself.'

As with Kenneth Branagh, there was once excitable talk of Callow being the man to inherit Laurence Olivier's crown. He winced when I mentioned it. 'That was absolute nonsense. It was never really on for me because I wasn't prepared to follow the conventional path. All that nonsense about starting out playing Hamlet and finishing off with Lear, just because one was supposed to, and because everyone else had, just bored me silly.'

Simon Callow was born in Streatham, London, on 15 June 1949.

Robert Hardy

Robert Hardy, if he were alive today, would have had something to say about the presumptuousness of any politician laying claim to being 'Churchillian'. The actor played the great wartime leader on innumerable occasions — most notably in the celebrated television series *Winston Churchill: The Wilderness Years* — but he always approached the part with deference and humility. 'The thing about Churchill is that people always sensed his greatness,' Hardy told me. 'That makes it enormously difficult to do him justice because an actor can never fake that. It has to come from within.'

The year was 1988 and Hardy was preparing to play Churchill in a musical called *Winnie*. Even in such straits, he was determined to retain his character's dignity, come what may. 'I've played him so many times, I've come to feel protective of him. I could have sat this one out, but I wouldn't have felt comfortable letting anyone else take on the role. I wanted to make sure it was done properly.'

Hardy professed to be no more than 'a middle-of-the road actor, lucky to be working'. There were, however, few, if any, parts he played in which he wasn't compelling. It wasn't, of course, just Churchill he made his own, but also Siegfried Farnon in the television series *All Creatures Great and Small*, and, later, Cornelius Fudge in the Harry Potter films. A Hardy performance was almost always big, flamboyant and just this side of being hammy. He was especially good at communicating raw fury. One thinks of the Robert Maxwell-like tycoon he played in *Inspector*

Morse. In person, the actor was, however, an anxious man. 'There hasn't been any role that's come easily to me,' he said. 'Real-life characters place additional responsibilities on an actor. I feel a compulsion to read everything I can about them, which, in the case of Churchill, meant it was a full-time occupation.'

He talked a lot about his old friend Richard Burton, whom he met at Oxford University and revered. It may well have been this proximity to such an exceptional actor at an early age that gave him his anxiety. 'I absolutely loved Rich, and, of course, he made me want to be a better actor every time I saw him on stage, but he had these unique gifts that I could never hope to compete with. He was a wonderful friend, but I do think sometimes that if I hadn't known him — hadn't seen him on stage so many times and been so close to that magic — I'd probably have been a lot more contented with my lot.' He must have been hurt when, a few years before his death, Burton's diaries were published and all his hero could think of to say about him was that he had lent Hardy a lot of money when he was struggling that he'd never repaid.

At the age of eighty-seven, Hardy courageously consented to play Churchill one last time in Peter Morgan's play *The*

Audience, which looked at the Queen's relationships with her prime ministers over the years. Hardy suffered cracked ribs in a fall in his home, and, after soldiering on for a whole week's preview performances, eventually decided the pain was too much and 'reluctantly' bowed out before the first night. He died four years later at Denville Hall, the home for retired actors.

Robert Hardy was born in Cheltenham on 29 October 29 1925, and died in Northwood, London, on 3 August 2017, aged ninety-one.

Robert Hardy played Henry V to Judi Dench's Princess Katherine in the BBC's *An Age of Kings* (1960).

Roy Dotrice & Patrick Garland

Roy Dotrice and Patrick Garland both found fulfilment in their marriages to, respectively, Kay and Alexandra, but they found it together, too, in *Brief Lives*. It was at the Hampstead Theatre in 1967 that Dotrice first appeared in Garland's adaptation of *The Memoirs, Miscellanies, Letters and Jottings of John Aubrey* that recounted the impressions a real-life seventeenth century Englishman had formed of the famous people he'd met in his day. The life of the show turned out to be anything but brief: on the West End, Broadway and around the world, Dotrice went on to portray Aubrey in more than 1,700 performances, which still warrants a mention in *Guinness World Records* as the longest-running one-man show ever staged.

In 2008, almost half a century on, Garland, then seventy-two, and Dotrice, at eighty-four, had taken it upon themselves to revive the play. I went to see the old troupers rehearsing in a draughty rehearsal hall just around the corner from Euston Station. For both men, this was clearly a labour of love. Dotrice, dressed in jeans, a Garrick tie and a blazer, was struggling with a gruesome cough, but was, with each line he uttered, slowly bringing back to life the old diarist that he and Garland had got to know so well.

Scarcely six months before, Dotrice's wife had died suddenly of a heart attack. They had been married for more than sixty years. It had, said Dotrice, been Kay's last wish that he should do the play. 'I'd never agree to

Roy Dotrice in ITV's drama series
Armchair Theatre — A Cold Peace (1965).

do anything without talking to her first. She was a great actress herself and always knew instinctively how parts should be played. I'd started reading it through with her in what turned out to be her final days. She felt I had become far too hammy in the part by the time I did my final performances in the role in 1974. I was chasing after the laughs too much. This time I am doing it the way she wanted — I'm going back to basics.'

He had been discussing the idea of reviving *Brief Lives* with Garland, the director of the original production as well as its creator, for several years. That they managed to secure a regional tour for it when they did had proved to be a 'godsend' for Dotrice, as it gave him a sense of direction and purpose when he desperately needed both. 'I think actors who play the same parts over a long period of time go one of two ways — either they switch to autopilot or they get into an ever more intimate relationship with the character,' he said. 'I have taken the second route. I think, too, now I've lived through so much more of what Aubrey was talking about — not least, bereavement — I have so much more to draw on.'

Dotrice and Garland brought a wealth of experience to the production. The former toured with the RSC and went on to pick up, among other glittering prizes, a Tony award for *A Moon for the Misbegotten* on Broadway in 2000 and, remarkably, five Grammy nominations. On screen, he received particular acclaim for playing Mozart's domineering father in *Amadeus*. He also appeared in *The Scarlet Letter* with Demi Moore.

Garland, meanwhile, was a former artistic director of the Chichester Festival Theatre. Notable successes included *Forty Years On, A Doll's House* and *The Mystery of Charles Dickens,* with Simon Callow. On Broadway, he directed Rex Harrison in *My Fair Lady*. 'If you've managed to direct Rex and survive, there isn't a lot that frightens you,' said Garland. 'He had an explosive temper. Niamh Cusack once said to Edward Fox, as they were rehearsing *The Admirable Crichton,* that she was thinking of suggesting to Rex that he played a scene in a slightly different way. Edward said "I wouldn't do that if I were you". The cast then heard Niamh begin a conversation with Rex and he started off rather quietly — a bit like a tsunami gradually building up — and then suddenly you could hear him four blocks away as he screamed "if it's got to the point in my fucking career that I have to take acting lessons...".'

Happily, there were no temper tantrums rehearsing *Brief Lives*. 'We've actually got to the point that we know what we're both thinking before we even have to say it,' said Garland. 'It really is a bit like a marriage.' They were both conscious that they were making something of a statement with their wonderfully old-fashioned play. The challenge was to get audiences to share their enthusiasm. 'I believe there is always an appetite for plays that have something to say,' Garland said. 'That's all Roy and I want to do — to communicate with an audience.'

The two men are often surprised by how *Brief Lives* changed not just their lives, but so many of the people who saw it. Garland read in the *Daily Telegraph* how

Hugh Massingberd had, when he became the newspaper's obituaries editor, decided to try to illuminate the lives of great men through gossip and anecdote after seeing how well Aubrey had done it during the show's original run. Dotrice, for his part, recalled a middle-aged couple coming up to him on a railway station in 1969. 'They told me they had seen the play just before they had planned to emigrate to New Zealand. They realised they couldn't possibly leave the country because to do so would be to deny their history and their past. They decided to stay in this country as a result of seeing the play.'

In the event, *Brief Lives* toured the regional venues to good-natured reviews, but never made the West End transfer they'd set their hearts on. Garland told me how he and Dotrice both knew that the play was good and sometimes that had to be enough. 'I remember writing to Laurence Olivier to say how much I regretted my production of *Cyrano* had not got better reviews. Olivier replied that some of his greatest work had been torn to pieces by the critics and the public. And lots of work that he knew to be rubbish had been praised to the skies. Sometimes there is just no accounting for taste.'

Roy Dotrice was born on Guernsey on 26 May 1923, and died in London on 16 October 2017, aged ninety-four. Patrick Garland was born in London on 10 April 1935, and died in Worthing on 19 April 2013, aged seventy-eight.

Patrick Garland with his wife, Alexandra Bastedo.

Michael Hordern

When Richard Burton uttered the words 'Broadsword calling Danny Boy' on his transmitter in the film *Where Eagles Dare*, it was Michael Hordern who picked up at the other end. For a distinguished stage actor whose career spanned more than half a century — the King Lear he played at Stratford in 1969 was the stuff of legend — he was grimly reconciled to the fact he'd probably be most remembered for that endlessly repeated old war film.

'That was a particularly daft one, but, to be honest, I've never taken all that much satisfaction in any film as you can never really get into a character,' he told me. 'Just when you start to feel you are, someone shouts "cut", so it feels like trying to run a marathon in instalments. You can't get into your stride.'

I met Hordern in 1986 when, after losing his wife, Eve, a few months earlier, he lived in a cluttered flat high up in an old block in Chelsea. On the floor lay the damp pages of a script over which he'd just spilt a mug of coffee. He was then seventy-six and admitted he had never realised how hard his wife must have toiled to keep the place clean and tidy.

His year of personal loss had, however, seen a revival of his professional fortunes after he had a hit playing an eccentric old vicar in a television adaptation of Sir John Mortimer's *Paradise Postponed*. It seemed, however, to be little more than an encumbrance for him. His telephone was ringing off the hook with calls from journalists in

175

Australia where it was about to be screened. 'No, Sir
Michael isn't here,' he said emphatically to one caller in
his all-too-familiar voice.

I suggested we adjourn to a restaurant over the road
for a bite to eat. A bottle of Sancerre soon helped to make
him wonderfully indiscreet. He talked about all the things
actors aren't supposed to — doing advertisements ('I get
a twinge of guilt every time I do one, but they are so very
remunerative'), colleagues ('Rex Harrison was impossible
as a director — I nearly decked him'), job offers ('they want
me to do a play at Chichester, but I can't be bothered'),
and what a nightmarish time he'd had up at Stratford
during Sir Trevor Nunn's period in charge ('I've nothing

against Trevor, but, in all honesty, I didn't feel there was anyone on the bridge').

Of the very mannered performance of David Threfall, playing an unscrupulous politician in *Paradise Postponed*, he said: 'I'm not sure whether that sort of thing can really be called acting.' Committing perhaps the ultimate sacrilege, he even had a go at theatregoers. 'About four weeks into the run, there aren't any more intelligent audiences to be had. You get people laughing in all the wrong places and they're silent when something very funny has just been said. That's actually the main reason why I find a long run so exhausting. It isn't that I haven't the stamina. I haven't the ruddy patience.'

He let slip that he'd been offered the part of *Doctor Who* when William Hartnell gave it up, but he felt it wasn't his scene. The part he'd yearned for had been the title role in *Rumpole of the Bailey*, and, while its creator John Mortimer was a mate, it went instead to Leo McKern and he admitted he was 'heartbroken'. Still, he said he'd taken some consolation in narrating an animated BBC adaptation of Michael Bond's Paddington Bear books, which had been 'a lot of fun'.

The charming but slightly dotty characters that Hordern made his own on stage and screen were often not entirely unlike the man himself, but, touchingly, he kept apologising throughout our lunch for being boring. 'I don't mind at all being boring, even if it can be a bit of a strain on other people. I can only apologise. I think as an actor it's so much easier to assume someone else's character when you haven't got one of your own.'

Still, he said he had felt 'immensely gratified' when he overheard two little boys squabbling as he'd made a call in a telephone box. 'When I finally emerged,' he said, 'one of them asked me if I was by any chance Paddington bear.'

Sir Michael Hordern was born in Berkhamsted, Hertfordshire, on 3 October 1911, and died in Oxford on 2 May 1995.

Anthony Quayle

All actors have areas of their lives that are off limits and it was no different with Sir Anthony Quayle. For once, it had nothing whatever to do with his private life — he had found blissful happiness with his second wife, Dorothy Hyson — or a play or a film that had bombed so badly it was considered bad form to bring it up. Quayle had lately narrated a Conservative Party broadcast, and, under a prime minister quite as divisive as Margaret Thatcher, that was something that he knew wouldn't go down well with vast swathes of the public, not to mention a lot of his fellow actors. He knew, too, it would also complicate the public perception of his knighthood, which he had accepted the preceding year.

'If you don't mind, dear boy, I'd really rather not get into that,' he told me. 'It was just another job, that's all.'

Quayle may well have come to regret it as the Compass Theatre Company, which he'd founded four years previously, was struggling in Margaret Thatcher's Britain. The year was 1988, and, as he was overseeing rehearsals for Gogol's *The Government Inspector*, he had learnt that a sponsorship deal he thought had been signed and sealed had been cancelled because the company concerned had been taken over. 'We are such bloody philistines when it comes to the arts,' he said. 'Don't people realise that theatre is important to the health of society? It's about the only time we all still get together in one room, for goodness sake.'

He felt *The Government Inspector* symbolised everything that Compass was about. 'We're in the age of commercialism in theatre and this is the kind of play that wouldn't otherwise be done. The emphasis these days is on productions that guarantee their backers good returns, and, for that reason, we are losing a great deal of our theatrical heritage. You might say people have been saying that for generations, and, indeed, I remember Olivier saying it to me when I was in my twenties, but the danger really is greater now since the overheads in theatre are higher than they've ever been.'

Quayle was without question one of the greatest actors and directors of his day. He had helped to establish Stratford-upon-Avon as a major powerhouse of British theatre and won widespread acclaim for his Shakespearean roles and notable Broadway performances in *Tamburlaine the Great* in 1956, and *Galileo* in 1967. He appeared, too, in more than thirty films, including his Oscar-nominated turn as Cardinal Wolsey in *Anne of the Thousand Days* in 1970. There were also his fine film performances in war films such as *Ice Cold in Alex* and *The Guns of Navarone*. In real life, incidentally, he'd had an especially impressive war: he joined the Special Operations Executive and served as a liaison officer with the partisans in Albania.

The only fight that interested Quayle when we met was the one he was waging on behalf of his cast. 'Look at them,' he said, pointing to the members of his doughty little company as they rehearsed. 'They'll have to be away from home for three months on this run. It'll be bloody hard work and the pay will be terrible. I'm not asking for sympathy for them — they're professionals, they wouldn't want to be doing anything else. All I am saying is that I wish to God there was some way I could at least say to them their jobs are secure and the company will still be together in a year or so's time.'

Quayle said he was in the process of making way for younger blood at Compass. 'Rather like King Lear, but hopefully with better results,' he said, with a wry smile.

Sir Anthony Quayle was born in Southport, Lancashire, on 7 September 1913, and died in Chelsea, London, on 20 October 1989, aged seventy-six.

Stewart Granger

R ichard Burton had just filmed a scene with Stewart Granger for *The Wild Geese*. The Welsh actor was in a car being driven to the next location with Roger Moore. 'Richard turned to me and said, wearily "Why does Stewart always have to be such an unutterable shit?"' Moore recalled, years later. '"I mean, at the ages we all are now — why can't the bloody man just grow up?" I shook my head and said "That's just Stewart, he can't help it".'

Moore was more tolerant about Granger's hissy fits than Eleanor Parker, Granger's co-star in *Scaramouche*, who considered him to be 'a dreadful person, rude and just awful. Everyone disliked him. Just being in his presence was bad.' Sir Christopher Lee told me how he remembered him making an inordinately long speech at some show business function and suddenly everyone had burst into laughter when Peter Cushing had plaintively said, when he finally finished, 'I suppose a cup of tea would be out of the question?'

Still, Granger was charm personified when I met him in 1990. A mane of brilliantined grey hair, a deep tan, gleaming white teeth, he looked, even at seventy-seven, every inch the Hollywood star. He was residing in California, but his friends Glynis Johns and Rex Harrison had persuaded him to return to his native Britain to make a stage comeback with them in a production of Somerset Maugham's *The Circle.* That pair's ill health and death

Stewart Granger and Jean Simmons in *Footsteps in the Fog* (1955).

respectively meant he had become the only member of the original cast still standing for the West End transfer. I'd innocently wondered if it was to honour Harrison's memory that he wanted to go ahead with the play's run. 'No, it's money,' he said, with a broad smile. 'It's always money. I don't ever work for the love of it.'

If Granger was in a very bad mood making most of his films, it was almost certainly because he didn't really regard acting as a fit and proper job for a grown man. 'If I was a more sensible human being, I'd have done something worthwhile with my life and become a doctor. My problem is I like a certain kind of lifestyle that requires money. People ask me sometimes how I could have appeared in such terrible films. The answer is always the same — money, money, money.'

In his later years, the critics had started to discern new depths in some of Granger's performances, but he saw that as ironic rather than satisfying. 'It's rare for an actor to have looks and talent at the same time. Usually the talent comes after the looks have gone — when it's not an awful lot of use as no one's watching any more.'

Acting just seemed to make him unhappy and every story he told me was to make light not of himself, but what he did for a living. The funniest of these was his account of how Elvis Presley had once come up to him in a restaurant. 'He said he'd seen me in *King Solomon's Mines* more than sixty times. I told him I was flattered. Elvis then shook his head sadly and added: "I didn't have any choice in the matter, Mr Granger. You see, at the time I was working as an usher in a cinema where the godawful film was playing."'

Stewart Granger was born in Kensington on 6 May 1913, and died in Santa Monica, California, on 16 August 1993, at the age of eighty.

Charlton Heston

Charlton Heston was appearing on the London stage as Sir Thomas More in *A Man for All Seasons*. The actor was a big guy in a wig whose views on everything from gun control to gay rights had made him politically incorrect before the term had even been invented. Henry VIII's Lord Chancellor was a man of great sensitivity, and it was this side of Heston that his publicist had, somewhat optimistically, suggested I explore.

This was 1987 when Heston wasn't fashionable among the chattering classes. There was still, however, something about the sixty-two-year-old star of epics like *Ben-Hur* and *The Ten Commandments* — in which he'd played Moses — that made him hard to ignore. He'd checked into the Dorchester and there was a queue of journalists waiting outside his capacious suite. When I was finally ushered into his presence, it was clear that finding his 'sensitive side' was going to be challenging. He was in a foul temper as the reviews for his performance had not all been adulatory.

'It's the mean-spiritedness of some of your critics that gets to me,' Heston began, before I'd even asked a question. 'They are all liberals and if the sons-of-bitches were honest, they'd admit it's my politics they were sitting in judgement upon, not my acting. I didn't expect any favours, but blind hatred is well out of order. I mean,

coming here to do this play, I hardly even cover my expenses; there's no gratitude.'

Still, in terms of the bigger picture, Heston couldn't complain. His old friend Ronald Reagan was in his second term as president, and, so far as he was concerned, his country was starting to stand every bit as tall as he was. He approved mightily, too, of Margaret Thatcher as our prime minister. 'I'm sick of the scroungers, sick of the people who want a free ride,' he said.

I noticed a spare wig on a table in an adjoining room, and, if I am honest, I didn't take him as seriously as I should. I suppose I saw him as a shouty man from another time and simply couldn't see that the tide was starting to change in favour of rich, white men like him. Heston got something I had still to come to terms with, which is to say that politics and show business had started to become inextricably linked and the right had learnt to become a lot more entertaining than the left.

'America has been afraid of its own shadow for too long and pandered to every crackpot special interest group in its midst, but now, thanks to Ronnie, it's standing up for itself again and looking after its own best interests,' Heston told me. 'I'm proud that a member of my profession is now leading the free world. There's no more important part of the job so far as I am concerned than communicating and that's what Ronnie knows all about.'

Heston talked so much about politics that I asked him why he had never himself stood for elected office. 'I haven't the temperament for it and I certainly haven't the patience,' he growled. 'I'd almost certainly have ended up decking some of my opponents, and, frankly, they'd have deserved it.'

If Heston had lived to see the Trump presidency — and the shift to the far right that Brexit represented here — he'd almost certainly have approved, but I doubt it would have made him any less angry. There would still have been the gnawing sense of grievance that he was never accorded the respect he felt was his due as an actor.

Charlton Heston was born in Wilmette, Illinois, on 4 October 1923, and he died in Beverly Hills on 5 April 2008, aged eighty-four.

Kirk Douglas

Kirk Douglas was seventy-three when I met him — still virtually his infancy given how many more years he had yet to live — and he was promoting his first novel *Dance With the Devil*. All the big Hollywood stars reach a point when there is no territory in their lives that has been untrodden by journalists. The chances of a veteran like Douglas telling a story that he had not told a hundred times before were therefore remote, and the only interest really lay in the form of words and the nuances he'd employ when he looked back on his over-analysed life and times.

He was staying at the Dorchester in London in a vast suite overlooking Hyde Park and there was the usual queue of journalists waiting to see him. The guy who'd been in before had had a dimple on his chin, and, as he was leaving, Douglas was telling him that no one who had a dimple could be all bad. I was led in by the public relations woman and Douglas jumped up to shake my hand, and, immediately seeing I was dimpleless, I could almost see him mentally preparing himself for the fact that I might indeed be all bad.

Maybe Douglas's classic newspaper drama *Ace in the Hole* — in which he played a hack willing to let a guy die to further his career — had given him a bit of an attitude to journalists. I probably didn't help matters by trying to be a bit edgy and asking him avant-garde questions intended to provoke. Did he ever get sick of having to be Kirk Douglas all the time? 'No,' he replied. If he'd been a

187

Kirk Douglas and his wife, Anne Buydens.

critic, would he ever have been minded to give himself a bad review as an actor? 'No,' he replied. Isn't insanity a necessary prerequisite to long-term stardom? 'No,' he replied.

So I decided to go for the jugular, and, mindful that Michael Douglas had for so long always been referred to as Kirk Douglas's son, I wondered how the patriarch felt — this was post *The Streets of San Francisco* and films like *Wall Street* and *Fatal Attraction* — that he'd started to be referred to as Michael's father. Did he ever by any chance succumb to just the tiniest amount of professional jealousy? 'No,' he replied.

All these questions had seemed very clever when I'd thought them up, but they were getting me nowhere, so I'd no alternative but to resort to raising his paint-by-numbers novel about a middle-aged film director falling in love with a former prostitute. He'd had a big success with his memoirs *The Ragman's Son* and I wondered if he found writing a work of fiction more or less of a challenge.

This finally elicited an answer that was not monosyllabic. 'I saw this novel like a film: it was a series of scenes, one after the other. I saw it as my job to describe the scenes and that's what I did.' I cheekily asked him if he'd availed himself of the services of a ghostwriter. 'Yes, my publishers offered me one, but I told them that if the ghost was as good as they said he was, they should get him to do his own damn book.'

If he had his life over again, I wondered, might he have focused more on writing than acting? This, alas, elicited another 'no'. The public relations woman came in, tapped her watch insistently, and said I'd only got another two minutes. I suspected there'd been a panic button somewhere close to Douglas that he'd pressed to indicate to her he'd had enough of my insolence.

I glanced down at my notes — the word 'no' written in shorthand over and over again — and realised this had not been one of my greatest moments. I finally asked Douglas, as I was leaving, if he thought, if I were ever to interview him again, he could envisage answering 'yes' to any of my questions. 'No,' he replied, and finally we both laughed. If only I'd had a dimple.

Kirk Douglas was born in New York on 9 December 1916, and died in Beverly Hills on 5 February 2020, aged 103.

Rod Steiger

In a kinder, gentler time in journalism — and in show business — I used to phone the press office of The Savoy and ask if they had anyone staying who'd make a good interview. No PR people, no money exchanging hands, just a quick call to the star's suite and they either wanted to do it or they didn't. And so it was I met Rod Steiger.

This was an actor whose career had come in distinct stages: Marlon Brando's brooding young co-star in *On the Waterfront; In the Heat of the Night*'s world-weary cop defining him in middle age; and then came the wilderness years when the shouty priest in *The Amityville Horror* could probably be regarded as a high point. In 1988, when I took the lift to his suite, he was sixty-three and probably best known for getting married — a feat he managed five times — and appearing on chat shows.

It was midday and he greeted me in his dressing gown, a slightly lop-sided wig and the news that he was going to marry his present wife — Paula — once again. 'I was on anti-depressants when I married her at Marylebone Register Office two years ago and I hardly knew what was going on. This time I want to do it properly, so I can remember it.'

He was in town to hear Anna, his daughter by Claire Bloom, sing at Covent Garden. Paula, his intended — I suppose, more accurately, his re-intended — was out shopping and the actor best known for his tough guy roles had about him an air of melancholia and vulnerability. His industry was, he admitted, getting him down.

Rod Steiger and Sydney Poitier in *In the Heat of the Night* (1967).

'It's into a lean period. It's apparently felt that there is no longer a market for films that have something to say and certainly no one wants to say anything new. I just heard they're going to make a mini-series out of *In the Heat of the Night*. It smacks of disinterment.'

The new generation of actors he saw coming up did not impress him. 'I speak to them sometimes. All they want is to be stars. When actors of my generation were starting out, all we wanted was to do a good play. The public, too, don't seem to want to stick with anyone any more. There's this terrible need for new faces. I look around at the young stars we have now and I honestly wonder how many of them will still be around in twenty years.'

Steiger was aware that he had himself got stuck in a rut. 'You get to realise, after you've been in acting for a while, that you're just a commodity. People expect certain things of a Rod Steiger part, in the way they expect certain things of a brand of washing powder. Of course, it's depressing.'

I asked Steiger if he felt it was wise to talk about his depression and he said he was past caring. 'There were eight years of my life when it pretty much incapacitated me. Honestly, there were days I just didn't get out of bed.

People see it as a weakness, but it's a medical condition. A chemical imbalance in the body. We're never going to understand it — still less work out how to fix it — if we don't talk about it.'

Steiger was never exactly a looker, but he was a mesmerising screen and stage presence and I've no doubt his internal demons were a factor in that. He'd been raised a Lutheran, but had come to the view that there was no God. He said that had made his performance as Pontius Pilate in Franco Zeffirelli's *Jesus of Nazareth* important to him.

'Pilate's big line, when he says to Jesus, "what is the truth?" well, that's really the whole problem humanity has to face. What the hell is it? Why are we all here? What's the point? Jesus never did give him an answer and there's never, so far as I can see, been one since.'

Then Steiger yawned, said he hadn't slept at all the night before, and would I mind very much if that was that as he'd decided to head back to bed.

Rod Steiger was born in Westhampton, New York, on 14 April 1925, and died in Los Angeles on 9 July, 2002, aged 77.

Rod Steiger and Diana Dors in *The Unholy Wife* (1957).

Claire Bloom

Occasionally stars give performances that are so convincing it's hard to disentangle them from the people they really are. There are few better examples of this than Claire Bloom's glacially cold Lady Marchmain in the television adaptation of *Brideshead Revisited*. I realised as I knocked on her dressing room door that I was psyching myself up to meet her ladyship. The Miss Bloom inside still retained the character's poise and elegance, but it became clear soon enough that she was contrastingly human, fallible and likeable.

This was when she was seventy-five and preparing for a West End play called *Six Dance Lessons in Six Weeks*. She was conscious that a run lasting several months was going to require her to 'ration' her energy. I was lucky to see her, as she had chosen to expend it on very few interviews. The only ground rule she had set was she wasn't willing to talk about politics. 'What this or that actor thinks about politics is really neither here nor there,' she said. 'Who cares? I most sincerely hope no one takes any notice when they do start talking about such matters.'

That is not to say she'd ever held back when talking about herself. In her memoirs *Leaving a Doll's House*, she recounted with blistering honesty her bitter divorce from the writer Philip Roth. She'd even admitted that to try to salvage the relationship, she'd thrown Anna, her teenaged daughter from her union with Rod Steiger, out of their house. 'Philip had given me an ultimatum, but I shouldn't have got into that in the book. I was ill-advised. There are some things it's better to keep private. Anna and I have, however, come through it. She's now distinguished herself in the world of opera and I regard her as my best friend.'

Bloom had no wish to see or hear from Roth again. He cost her a great deal, not least in therapists' bills. 'It took ten years for me to come to terms with what happened, but now I can evolve the experience into something that's positive.' I noted that all the men in her life had happened to be famous: Laurence Olivier, Richard Burton, Anthony Quinn and Yul Brynner. There were also, of course, her three husbands: in addition to Steiger and Roth, she had, for a time, been married to the producer Hillard Elkins.

With no formal education to speak of — she had been shunted from school to school during the war years — she said she deliberately sought out intelligent and successful men. 'I learnt a lot from all of them and that was what I wanted. They kept me on my toes. It was exciting and I've always looked for excitement in my life, and, goodness knows, I found it.' She'd once been quoted as saying that women, when they are involved with great men, always have to 'fight for their existence', and had added, darkly, that all the most accomplished artists are also, by definition, monsters. 'I think if I said that I must have been thinking about a specific experience in my life. I am sure some great artists are very dangerous to women — one thinks of Picasso — but not all of them.'

In *Six Dance Lessons in Six Weeks,* her character observes 'everyone pays for sex, one way or another', and that struck her as very true. 'We always pay an emotional price,' she said. I asked her if it had ever been too high for her. 'I'm still here, so I would say it has been fair,' she replied. I suggested that maybe the greatest and most satisfying relationship of her life had been with acting and she did not demur. I wondered why that was. 'I seem somehow to have kept alive in me that sense of wonder that we all have when we are children and we pretend to be someone we are not,' she answered.

Claire Bloom was born in Finchley, Middlesex, on 15 February 1931.

Eartha Kitt

T he night before I interviewed Eartha Kitt, I went to see her in *Follies*. That 1988 production is now regarded as one of the greatest ever stagings of Stephen Sondheim's musical and its star's rendition of the big number *I'm Still Here* was a showstopper.

'There's a line in it that goes "Good times and bum times, I've seen 'em all, and, my dear, I'm still here" and I guess that amounts to a fair enough summary of my life,' she said. 'I've certainly known bum times. I'm neither black nor white, so, in the early days in America, I had just about everybody on my back. The CIA ran a smear campaign against me, saying I was a nymphomaniac, but, you know, I can count the men I'd been with on the fingers of one hand.'

Her father was a farmer about whom she knew little. He had deserted her mother, a Cherokee of African descent, when she was barely two. The young Eartha had started out in night clubs and got her break in 1950 when Orson Welles saw her performing and cast her as Helen of Troy in his version of the Faust story, *Time Runs*. He considered her to be 'the most exciting woman in the world'. I asked if they'd ever been lovers. 'No,' she replied.

She went on to gain acclaim as an actress and singer — notable hits included *C'est si bon* and *Santa Baby*. Her films included *St Louis Blues*, with Nat King Cole; *Anna Lucasta,* with Sammy Davis Jr; and *Dragonard,*

Eartha Kitt and Cesar Romero in *Batman* (1966).

with Oliver Reed. Probably it was Catwoman in the 1960s television series *Batman* that defined her for a generation of youngsters.

We were lunching *al fresco* on a hot summer's day in Covent Garden. She was wearing thick sunglasses that covered a large expanse of her face. She explained in that distinctively feline voice of hers that they had nothing to do with the sun. She'd been involved in a road accident the month before and had needed twenty stitches. There was no question of her pulling out of the show. 'You get offered so much crap that when something as great as this comes along, you can't allow anything to stop you,' she said. 'After that crash, I got out of the car with blood all over me and all I could think about was whether the scar was going to be visible from the stalls.'

I could see what Welles had found so exciting about her. It was the fact she was so completely unaffected. She'd suddenly lean across the table and gather up my salad in her hands and transfer it, without explanation, to her plate. When one of my questions bored her, she'd let me know by taking out her tapestry and beginning, quite implacably, to weave.

Performing, however, clearly mattered to her, and so did her causes. She was a gay rights campaigner in the days when that still raised eyebrows and so much of what she said during her career shows she understood the objectives of Black Lives Matter, decades before the movement was founded. 'I love a lot of gays, I love a lot of black people; what am I supposed to do when I see them being victimised? Just sit back and say "what the hell?"'

After we'd had our coffees, a man hovered beside our table and she turned towards him and scowled. 'I am Eartha Kitt and I am trying to do an interview,' she snapped at him. The man replied courteously that he was the owner of the restaurant and he just wanted her to know how proud he was to have her as a patron and the meal was on the house. She finally took off her glasses, revealing all of her stitches, and smiled at him. 'Oh, I am so sorry, I just get tired of it all sometimes,' she told him. 'It's only when you're as old as I am that you get to see how ridiculous this whole show business thing is.'

As she headed back to the theatre to prepare for the evening's performance, she turned to me and said 'you'll figure me out one day'. I said I reckoned I had. 'You're only in your twenties. You can't even begin to, darling.'

Earth Kitt was born in South Carolina on 17 January 1927, and died in Connecticut on 25 December 2008 aged eighty-one.

David Frost

S ir David Frost met me in his office in a quiet little mews in Kensington. 'This is my *Daily Mail* week,' he said, as we sat down. 'Tomorrow I am having lunch with Sir David English.'

It was classic Frost that he should have felt the need to let me know he was meeting the chairman of the parent company of the newspaper for which I then worked. The message was clear: 'don't mess with me, sonny.'

Frost had achieved a great deal in his life — his famous interviews with Richard Nixon; groundbreaking Sixties satire, such as *That Was the Week That Was*; and he was one of the founders of the breakfast television outfit, TV-am, but, for all that, he never overcame his insecurity.

I happened to know someone who worked with Frost at TV-am and he said what struck him was that, for Frost, it was always about Frost. All that seemed to interest him when they had their editorial conferences was the size of the typeface for his name in the opening credits, how much promotion his interviews were going to get, were any of his fellow presenters being bigged up more than him? There was not even an attempt to give the impression he was part of a team.

It was the mid-1990s and all around his office there were photographs to reiterate the point that Frost was important: there he was with President Clinton, Nelson Mandela, Margaret Thatcher and then there were the awards that he had received. Interviews that he gave were always guarded, the lines he came out with had usually been said a hundred times before, but then great interviewers seldom, if ever, make great interviews. They know all the tricks.

I asked him if he felt, after all the cutting-edge television shows he had done, that presenting a bland daytime television show like *Through the Keyhole* was beneath him. 'Of course not,' he retorted. 'It's an enormously popular series, and, at the end of the day, I'm about making television that people want to watch.'

Nothing has ever come easy to Frost. Even securing his interview with Nixon, he had to outbid the American networks and put up his own money, which meant him selling his LWT shares — he had been involved in the creation of the company — which later soared when the company was taken over. At Cambridge, he was a grammar school boy who was subjected to a great deal of snobbery and this may well have given him his need to prove himself.

He was the secretary of the university's Footlights Drama Society, which brought him into close contact with Peter Cook, who appeared to treat him with derision. Another contemporary, the future journalist Christopher Booker, described him as a character it was 'impossible not to dislike' because he was so obviously desperate.

Frost yearned for Cook's approval, but it never came. When, in later life, he telephoned Cook to invite him to a dinner party he was hosting in several months' time for Prince Andrew and Sarah Ferguson, Cook said, 'Hang on, I'll just check my diary. Oh dear, I find I'm watching television that night.' Frost had appeared in several films — invariably as a journalist — such as *The VIPs* — and he appeared opposite Lucille Ball in an episode of *Here's Lucy*, but he was not, by any standards, a natural performer in the way that, say, Cook was, and nor did he possess his 'funny bones'.

Attempting to psychoanalyse Frost never got anywhere, and he would always give the answers he wanted to give,

David Frost with Richard Nixon, 37th President of the United States.

even if they bore no relation whatsoever to the questions. Inquiring, about failures he had been associated with — he was, in the late seventies, involved in producing an epic disaster film about the Loch Ness monster called *Nessie* that had to be abandoned — again drew a look of incomprehension. It was the same with a planned remake of *The Dam Busters* that he had attempted to produce.

Frost had no time for the suggestion that he had become too soft an interviewer, but it troubled him that political interviews were now a lot shorter than they were. 'Hour-long interviews with politicians were once routine, whereas now they seldom go on for much longer than ten minutes which gives little opportunity to stress-test their ideas,' he said. 'It's true I've never been an interviewer who goes in hard at the start because I've always taken the view you don't get what you want that way. John Smith, as Labour leader, used to say that I had a way of asking beguiling questions with potentially lethal consequences.'

I asked Frost finally if he was happy and felt valued and he paused for a few moments and said, yes, of course he was. 'I have achieved everything I've set out to achieve, so why wouldn't I?'

Sir David Frost was born in Tenterden, Kent, on 7 April 1939 and died from heart failure aboard the MS Queen Elizabeth, *on 31 August 2013, at the age of seventy-four.*

Malcolm Muggeridge

alcolm Muggeridge — 'St Mugg,' as he was known in his day — admitted to me that he had been an actor all of his life. His credits included *I'm All Right Jack* and *Heavens Above!* and what was striking about his appearances in those classic films was how seamlessly they welded with his television journalism.

'Guilty as charged,' he cried out when I put it to him that 'Malcolm Muggeridge' was no more than a part he'd played for pecuniary gain. When I asked him who he really was, he needed a few moments. 'Now that's not so easy to answer,' he said, eventually. 'As one grows older, and one sees one's life in perspective, one realises it's not a question that matters all that much.'

Journalists as entertainers have always been among us. I've seen Sir Robin Day playing himself very adroitly in a *Morecambe and Wise*, and newsreaders, such as Simon McCoy who appeared as himself in the film *Stormbreaker*, have long made it pretty obvious that what they do for a living is also just another form of acting. Boris Johnson, as a journalist and subsequently, has maybe taken performance art to a whole new level.

I met Muggeridge three years before his death when he was eighty-four and living in a cottage in Robertsbridge in Sussex with his wife Kitty. The encounter haunts me as he has posthumously been accused of being a 'compulsive groper' during his early days working for the BBC, a charge that his family accepted, although they were insistent that he later mended his ways.

Of Kitty, Muggeridge told me that she had always been 'the real saint' in the relationship. I wish now I'd pressed him more on why he'd said that, but he seemed aware that he'd not handled his personal life well. He'd married Kitty in 1927 when her father, a well-to-do colonel, shouted out from the back of the register office 'You can still get away, Kit'. Muggeridge admitted: 'Kitty's father could see through me. I had some odd ideas about marriage at first. I believed that we should be allowed our freedom.'

He insisted it was 'only talk' and that neither of them ever actually took other lovers, but he went on to say he did not consider himself to be, in terms of his adopted faith, 'a good Catholic'. Indeed, he said he'd felt so repulsed by himself, he'd tried committing suicide during the war when he had been working undercover in Mozambique. 'I got sick of it all and swam out to sea late one night, but, when I glanced back, the bright lights of the city made me want to come ashore again.'

I asked him if his controversial opinions — he had, for instance, made an intemperate attack on the Queen — were just a way of drawing attention to himself. 'I don't think I was ever controversial for the sake of it. I've never felt the Queen is the slightest use to anybody and I believe that fervently. I've nothing against her personally, of course.'

He had what he called a deep-rooted hatred of 'humbug' and that was why he'd fallen out with *The Guardian*, where he'd worked as their leader writer. 'C P Scott was then its editor and he made a great thing about how his paper would never carry advertisements for alcohol and bookies because he said they were immoral. He would never admit, however, that it was advertisements like those in what was then *The Guardian*'s sister paper — the *Manchester Evening News* — that was keeping his unprofitable paper afloat.'

His flirtation with communism had also ended in disillusionment when he travelled to Russia in the early 1930s and found the authorities indifferent to a major famine in Kiev. He said it was the last straw for him at *The Guardian*, when

Scott toned down the furious reports he filed. 'I've tried most of life's "isms" — Catholicism, Communism and journalism — with varying degrees of success,' he said.

Then he asked me something that took me aback: 'Do you ever think of becoming a journalist?' Having sat beside him for more than an hour writing down what he'd said in my notebook — and having made it clear on the phone a few days earlier I was interviewing him for a newspaper — I have to admit I found the question charming. I could have been any old herbert who'd wandered in for a chat and a cup of tea and yet he'd been so welcoming.

Malcolm Muggeridge was born in Sanderstead, Surrey, on 24 March 1903, and died in Robertsbridge, East Sussex, on 14 November 1990, aged eighty-seven.

Billy Graham

As a venerable democracy, Britain used to take a condescending view of America and the way she liked to wave her flag and loudly profess her faith in God. It wasn't that we were by and large unpatriotic or ungodly, but we just felt that we'd reached a point — certainly in the political arena — when we didn't need to be so demonstrative.

Still, at least no prime minister has (so far) felt the need to appoint a high-profile spiritual adviser. That was the role that the late Dr Billy Graham fulfilled for every president from Harry S Truman to Barack Obama.

I got to interview Graham when he was a sprightly seventy and preparing to go on a UK-wide crusade that was to culminate in a rally in London, where he addressed an audience of a quarter of a million people, and, via satellite links, tens of millions more around the world. I found him intriguing, but then I've always been drawn to actors, and that is what he was in so many respects.

He was turned out in a well-cut suit, the hair was coloured and the face discreetly made-up for my photographer. He knew exactly what he was doing and anyone who had ever seen him perform knew, of course, how he could connect with an audience every bit as effectively as Laurence Olivier.

I never doubted for one moment his faith, however, and, while American television evangelists have since often become mired in scandal, nothing ever stuck to Graham. When two good-looking members of his staff joined us

Former US presidents, George H W Bush, Bill Clinton and Jimmy Carter, with Billy Graham (centre) and his son, Franklin.

and said it had been a 'wild night', it didn't occur to me for one moment that they were talking about anything other than the weather.

On feminism, homosexuality and even, at the outset of his ministry, segregation, Graham was behind the curve, but then he was very much a product of his time. He was also unnervingly direct. 'In my Bible, sir, it lists the Ten Commandments and not the ten suggestions,' he told me, when I asked if he could ever see his way to forgiving someone who might have had a fleeting extra-marital affair, or even just told the mildest white lie. 'I am only a man, not a particularly intelligent man at that, but what I do understand is that it is the word of the Lord that matters, and it's not for me to try to reinterpret it to spare anyone's blushes.'

As for his own showmanship, he was unrepentant. 'I know a great many preachers who see a virtue in addressing small congregations in a way that's simple and unshowy, and, believe me, I have the greatest respect for them, but they can't, in all honesty, blame me for wanting to spread the Word of the Lord to the maximum number of people.'

Graham drove himself hard and certainly he knew when he took on his job the word 'retirement' wasn't mentioned in the terms and conditions. 'But I do not mind as I have read my Bible and I do not recall a single instance of a Prophet of the Lord saying, upon attaining the age of sixty-five, that he had done his time and was heading off for his place by the seaside to wind down.'

I found him funny and charming and also, in his utter conviction, impressive. He changed the lives of a great many. Sir Cliff Richard said it was at one of his rallies that he first publicly declared himself to be a Christian. Sir David Barclay, the late *Telegraph* owner, told me he'd been 'mesmerised' every time he'd seen him speak. My friend Bill Kenwright, the theatre impresario, said he took the pledge not to drink alcohol when, as a youngster, he had heard him lay down the challenge to his audience.

When he died, Graham was permitted to lie in honour at the United States Capitol rotunda in Washington, D C. It's telling that he proved irreplaceable in American public life.

Dr Billy Graham was born on 7 November 1918, in Charlotte, North Carolina, in the United States, and died on 21 February 2018, at the age of ninety-nine.

Cliff Richard

One of the frustrations of being Sir Cliff Richard is that newspapers invariably dispatch full-time show business journalists to talk to him. That's limiting for him, and limiting, too, for the public in terms of their understanding of him. It therefore delighted the veteran entertainer when, in 2006, Matthew d'Ancona, as editor of *The Spectator*, asked me to do the honours.

Sir Cliff and I had a wide-ranging conversation in which we spoke mostly about politics. 'I'm enjoying this,' he said. 'You haven't asked me once about *Summer Holiday* or even *Bachelor Boy*, which is a first.' The very fact Sir Cliff has managed to last as long as he has attests to his business acumen as much as his abilities as a performer. He has also always been something of a politician — he knows instinctively what to say and when — which may have made it natural for him to empathise with Tony Blair during the darkest days of his premiership.

Sir Cliff was headline news at the time because he had given the Blairs the run of his vast villa on Barbados as he felt they needed some respite after the Iraq war. 'I had watched Tony wither when that war got started,' Sir Cliff said. 'I saw him on television and it seemed to me he was suffering the results of his decision. I just felt sorry for him, and so I got in touch with Cherie and said: "Look, I don't do this sort of thing normally, but I just know my place on Barbados isn't going to be full of people this August and if you want to use it, then go

ahead." It was just something I wanted to do for him as a human being.'

Sir Cliff was then sixty-five, the age when most men have completed the metamorphosis into a fully-formed Victor Meldrew. It was striking, however, that he seldom, if ever, harped on about the past and never moaned. He was then — and I am sure still is — a man who lived determinedly in the present.

Still, listening again to my tape of the conversation, there were moments when he started to sound like a prototype Brexiter. 'It worries me a little bit that we don't stand up for our country and what we believe in, in the way that we used to. Whether we believe in it or not, our whole country is based very much on a Christian set of values and it seems to me that's something to be proud of, in that it has got us this far. I would naturally feel disappointed if we were to dump all of that... but that is not really happening, is it? It is not being dumped, it is just being pushed aside a little bit.'

That last qualification was typical Sir Cliff. He seemed incapable of becoming really angry about anything. He had an ability always to see things in perspective, and, indeed, he has since let it be known that, had he not become a resident of Barbados, he would have voted Remain in the EU referendum.

Sir Cliff has lately turned eighty and he's still performing. That, as he said to me, is life itself to him. Since I met him, he has had to go through the trauma of the unfounded allegations of child sexual abuse, but I've no doubt it was his Christian faith — the same that made him extend a hand of friendship to the Blairs — that sustained him. He has, of course, always sought to be the man he believes his fans want him to be, even now, which cannot always be easy. Still, the Peter Pan of pop has turned out to be tougher than a lot of us gave him credit for.

Sir Cliff Richard was born in Lucknow, British India, on 14 October 1940.

Rowan Atkinson

I met Rowan Atkinson on an autumn day in 1988 that, he informed me, was the tenth anniversary of the start of his career in show business. Up until that point, his credits included the groundbreaking satirical television series *Not the Nine O'Cock News, Blackadder* and its sequels, a couple of solo revues in the West End and on Broadway, the lead in Larry Shue's play *The Nerd*, and a cameo in the unofficial James Bond entry, *Never Say Never Again.*

Atkinson was then trying to gain acceptance as a serious actor in a production of the Chekhov classic *The Sneeze*, with Timothy West as his co-star. He had been rehearsing in a small hall in Chelsea, just across from the Thames, and we'd found a bench in a park to sit on. He was then thirty-three, nervous, awkward and unable to engage in eye contact. I'd hoped he'd make me laugh when we met, but he didn't, not once. 'People think because I can make them laugh on the stage, I'll be able to make them laugh in person,' he explained, apologetically. 'That isn't the case at all. I'm essentially a rather quiet, dull person, who just happens to be a performer.'

Entertaining the masses was a skill that seemed to come effortlessly to him, but gaining approval in more highbrow circles was proving elusive. Frank Rich, the powerful *New York Times* critic, had said in a review that Atkinson couldn't seem to progress beyond a 'fondness for toilet humour' and his act was based on an 'obsession with alimentary byproducts'.

Rowan Atkinson in ITV's *Maigret*.

Atkinson's days at a minor public school on the
Cumbrian coast had actually passed by unremarkably —
quite academic, no good at games, certainly not the sort
of embryonic comedian who'd regale his classmates with
funny stories — and he'd emerged, he said, 'with no hang-
ups' of the kind that had troubled Rich. The assumption
was that he'd become an electrical engineer, as it was for
that he'd been training.

'I never had a driving ambition to perform, but, when I
got to Oxford, there was an ad in the news sheet for the
dramatic society and I just thought I'd give it a go. I'd
always enjoyed acting in school plays, but never thought
of it as a career. I guess I would probably be with some
am-dram group now — and I'm sure quite happy — if the
right people hadn't taken an interest in me.'

As things started to progress, he fretted about how
his mother might take it. The family were staunch

Conservatives and his two older brothers had started in 'sensible jobs' in the City and working for a big company. 'I think my mother thought show business was full of bouncing cheques and homosexuals and people in nasty bow ties,' he said. 'I tried to reassure her by getting a really well-dressed, middle-class agent who looked like a bank manager.'

His first major television appearance was in a pilot show for London Weekend Television called *Canned Laughter*, in which he was such a success he was offered his own series. He turned it down, however, feeling that he wasn't quite ready. Later, when he was appearing on *Not the Nine O'Clock News*, he was still not especially ambitious, feeling, as he put it, 'strangely apathetic' to what was going on around him.

For all that, he was provoking strong reactions. *The Guardian* startlingly called him a 'wanker' in print, which upset him. 'Then I found myself reading what some pop star loved and hated — it was one of those silly lists they do in newspapers — and my name appeared under the latter heading. I remember being very struck at the time that a man I had never met actually hated me. It was rather frightening.'

The characters the early Atkinson liked to portray were almost always flawed and unhappy individuals — an angry bigot in the raincoat, a closeted gay vicar, a duplicitous politician, an impatient man in a queue — but all of them, he insisted, were 'bizarre figments' of his imagination, and no more. Atkinson didn't seem to like where I was going with this line of questioning and said he had to get back to rehearsals. We kept talking as he headed to the hall, and I asked him finally if he was happy. He stopped, thought for a moment, and then replied: 'Yes... I think I am. I hope people will give me credit, however, for being more than just a face-puller.'

Rowan Atkinson was born in Consett, County Durham, on 6 January 1955.

Stephen Fry

One autumnal day in 2013, Tony Gallagher, who was then my editor at *The Daily Telegraph,* happened to mention that he'd had breakfast at The Wolseley restaurant in St James's, and, sitting not far from him, had been Stephen Fry and Andy Serkis, the actor best known for playing Gollum in *The Lord of the Rings* films. Waiting for his own guest to arrive, Gallagher had been struck by how Fry, deep in conversation with Serkis, appeared to be addressing his millions of followers on Twitter while not actually touching a single key on his mobile phone.

I duly wrote what I considered to be an unremarkable story in the newspaper's Mandrake diary, beneath the headline 'Does Stephen Fry write his tweets?' I had included a quote from Fry's people, which appeared to answer the question, explaining that he always wrote his own tweets, but that some of them were 'timed,' which meant he didn't actually have to write them in real time. Back then, I have to admit all of this was new to me — and to Gallagher, and, I'm sure, most of the newspaper's readers — but then, we'd only just discovered Twitter.

I'd headed out into the country that night for a few days off, blissfully unaware that a tsunami was gathering strength in Fry's north London home. A *BBC America* journalist who wrote about what then happened talked about how I was subjected to 'the frightening majesty of Stephen Fry in full rage'. The actor and comedian wrote a 1,000-word blog about me on Tumblr (I can no longer find

Stephen Fry and Hugh Laurie in ITV's *Jeeves and Wooster* (1990).

it online) in which he called me, among other things, a 'shiny-faced, arse-witted, human cockroach' and 'a creep from the inner ring of Satan's rectum'. As any good libel lawyer will tell you, this all amounts to no more than vulgar abuse and it's everyone's right to come out with it. Still, it inevitably provoked a lot of comment at the time, and, in a book about my interactions with stars, I don't in all honesty feel I can omit the most explosive one of the lot.

Warming to his theme in his blog, Fry went on to say that he no longer had any faith at all in print media. 'When I do a *The Hobbit: The Desolation of Smaug* press junket next week, for example, I will do no print media. When I have to offer some PR for an up-coming BBC 2 series on being gay around the world called *Out There:* no print media. No magazines and certainly no newspapers. And it's all because of people like Tim Walker.

'One of the chief glories of Twitter, from my point of view, is that it allows me to short-circuit loathsome bottom-feeders of his kind. If I do a TV chat show, or a radio interview people are free to think I'm a wanker, because at least it's me they're listening to or watching. Not some "profile" version of me filtered through the envious, mean-spirited spite of an arsehole journalist whose only attainment is the ability to sneer.'

Needless to say, the vast legions of keyboard warriors Fry had at his command saw this as the order to open fire, and, for a few weeks, the bombardment I took on Twitter was intense. If I'd a pound for every time I was called a cunt, I'd now be happily retired and living on the Bahamas.

When we'd engaged briefly at the start of that epic battle in cyberspace, I'd thought the best thing to do was to invite Fry out to lunch. I recognised he was bipolar, but it always seemed to me that more probably united — rather than divided — us. We both happen to be members of a London club where — if we keep to the rules — we're expected not to abuse each other, so I suggested we meet there. He responded that he'd filming commitments and couldn't take me up on the offer any time soon, but gamely said that he would be up for it and even suggested it could be fun. Around that time I'd had a kiss-and-make-up lunch with Hugh Bonneville, the *Downton Abbey* actor, at the same venue, and, while also aggrieved about something I'd written, we'd finished it with a handshake. Sadly, the lunch with Fry never happened, but, for the avoidance of doubt, the offer remains open.

Stephen Fry was born in London on 24 August 1957.

217

Glenda Jackson

I made the mistake of asking Glenda Jackson if she was happy. She snorted with derision. 'This obsession with being happy is one of the curses of Western civilisation,' she said. 'I want to experience all the tears as well as all the laughter, and the last thing I want to be is to be content. I need to be discontented; I need stress, I need crises. It is, simply, the way I am.'

The actress best known for films such as *Sunday Bloody Sunday, Women in Love* and the television series *Elizabeth R*, was, in 1999, playing the unglamorous real-life role of Under-Secretary of State at the Department of the Environment and Transport. She was then sixty-two and determined to be as unactressy as it was possible to be.

She insisted that, even at the height of her career in show business, she'd never exactly been light-headed. Indeed, when Bette Davis came on the phone to tell her she had won an Oscar for *A Touch of Class*, she said it meant very little to her. It was left to her mother, Joan, who had once worked as a shop cashier and was one of the few who could 'read' her daughter, to say that she could tell she was, underneath it all, dead chuffed.

The actress-turned-politician had been born in war-torn Merseyside when Joan and her husband, Harry, a bricklayer, had initially toyed with the idea of calling her Shirley, after Shirley Temple. The moment they looked at their baby, red-faced and shrieking furiously in her cot, they realised they had produced instead a Glenda.

Glenda Jackson (centre) with Laurie Metcalf (left), and Alison Pill in *Three Tall Women* (2018). Peter Hapak/*New York* Magazine.

'I was surrounded by female relatives because both sets of grandparents lived very close to us and the men were away fighting,' she recalled of her upbringing. 'The women were dealt a very mixed deck, but they always took the view that life was something you had to get on with. I think that gave me an attitude to life early on.'

Glenda found she could act in am-dram productions — Joan felt her daughter saw it as the only way she could express her emotions — and, after winning a scholarship to the Royal Academy of Dramatic Art, she started out in rep. She married Roy Hodges, a struggling actor like herself, in 1958, but their eighteen-year union was, inevitably, a stormy affair, doubtless not helped by Glenda's difficulties communicating.

Her success at the Oscars did for her marriage to Roy as he admitted it hurt his male pride to have a wife making so much more money than him. The marriage was finally dissolved in 1976 after it emerged that Glenda had been having an affair with Andrew Phillips, a lighting engineer she met on location making a film.

Glenda said they did their best to protect their son Daniel from the fallout. What they could not protect him from was what Glenda called 'a very drunk young man', who thrust a broken bottle into his face when he had tried to placate him in a pub. He underwent extensive surgery for deep facial wounds, but his left eye could not be saved. 'I was able to cope because Daniel could cope,' said Glenda. 'It helped a great deal that he had an uncle who had lost an eye in a road accident and he'd seen how he had managed to overcome that.'

It was hard to reconcile the Glenda I met at her home in her Hampstead and Highgate constituency with the Glenda who had once stripped naked in front of Richard Chamberlain in *The Music Lovers,* rolled around with Oliver Reed in a daring scene in *Women in Love*, and whipped a man with her two-foot-long hair in Peter Brook's controversial *The Marat/Sade*. I asked if it ever made her blush to see some of her old films. 'I haven't seen myself on the screen since the early seventies,' she said. 'I must say, at the time I found all of that talk about me as a sex symbol rather amusing, and, yes, flattering. It certainly never embarrassed me.'

Glenda said it was Margaret Thatcher who decided her to go into full-time politics. 'It was that speech when she said there was "no such thing as society" that did it. I walked into my closed French windows because I was in such a rage.' Was acting a help to her as a politician? 'There's no comparison between trying to get across a scriptwriter's lines and policies that you believe in. This is real life. I found as an actress that it was very easy indeed to act badly and inordinately difficult to act well. It's the same being a good constituency MP and being effective at the Department. All I have ever really wanted is to do my best. If I have a terror it is, perhaps, of letting myself down.'

Her son Daniel is now, somewhat improbably, a *Mail on Sunday* columnist.

Glenda Jackson was born in Birkenhead, Cheshire, on 9 May 1936.

John Mills

D arling, I just want you to know that, after this bloody boring dinner is over and we are alone together, I'm going to kiss every single part of your beautiful body and you're not going to stop me.' Even in old age, Sir John Mills was still devilishly romantic, and, once he'd scribbled these words down on his napkin, he asked the waiter to give it to his wife Mary, who was sitting opposite him at a black tie gathering at one of London's grand hotels.

'And you know what the silly clot did — despite the fact I was gesticulating wildly at him — he gave it not to my wife, but to the guest of honour, who only happened to be Princess Diana,' said Mills, roaring with laughter. 'She read the note and then looked at me briefly with a look of total horror on her face. I might add that, after the dinner was over, I'd never seen a woman leave a room so quickly.'

He was talking to me in his home in Denham in Buckinghamshire, and, even though he had starred in 120 films and had an Oscar on his mantelpiece (Best Supporting Actor for *Ryan's Daughter*), he could still laugh at himself. It was 1998 and he had lately celebrated his ninetieth birthday, but was still able to act young. 'You know I am virtually blind now,' he said. 'I can locate where people are from their voices and so I train these useless old eyes on them and they assume everything is fine. And I think a tie and a blazer always takes years off you, so, when people come round who don't know any better, they generally assume I'm still pretty much intact.'

Harry Andrews, Anthony Quayle, Sylvia Syms and John Mills in
Ice Cold in Alex (1958).

The day before we met, Mills had been invited at the last
moment to speak at a special event to celebrate the life of
his fellow actor Michael Denison. Of course, he rose to the
occasion, standing bolt upright on the stage at the Theatre
Royal Haymarket, having first requested clear directions
on where to look and when. 'Every word, of course, had
to be learnt because I can't read speeches any more,' he
said. 'Michael was a friend of mine and I just didn't feel
I could let him down.' He added matter-of-factly that he
had some speaking engagements coming up in the States
which meant an early morning start later in the week and
there was another film part he was in discussions about.
'I don't really know how not to be busy,' he said. 'It makes
me feel a bit of fraud if I ever see a day in my diary with
nothing planned.'

I asked him why he still felt so driven and he recalled
an evening when he was on leave from the army during

the war. He and his wife Mary were getting ready to head out for a dinner-dance at the Café de Paris in the heart of London. 'We were both dressed up and ready to hail a cab and I suddenly said to Mary that I didn't want to go. She said a little crossly: "well, fine, if that's how you feel, but why?" I replied: "I just don't know, but I know I don't want to go there." That night we went for a walk in Hyde Park and witnessed what turned out to be one of the worst bombing raids of the war. It was like the whole of the West End was ablaze. The next morning, I learned that a bomb had gone through the roof of the Café de Paris and exploded on the dance floor, killing almost everyone in the building.'

He said there were close friends of theirs who had gone to the dinner-dance — they were going to sit together — and he was left with a sense that he had to make the most of every moment that was left to him. 'I don't think I ever went into anything half-heartedly after that,' he said. 'Not marriage, fatherhood, friendship or my work. I mean, after the war, I knew a lot of theatre actors who went into films thinking it was all a bit beneath them because it was only the boards that they felt mattered. I went into it absolutely determined to do my best and to take all the work I could get.'

I asked him if he felt he was a star. 'I think it feels vain to use a word like that because so much of it is out of your hands. You have a face and a voice and a way of moving about that either works on film or it doesn't. It's got nothing to do with hard work. Cinemagoers can also be pretty capricious and so it's silly to think if you suddenly find one day your name on a film poster that you are a star. You're just bloody lucky.'

Sir John Mills was born in Norfolk on 22 February 1908, and died in Denham, Buckinghamshire, on 23 April 2005, aged ninety-seven.

José Ferrer

Stardom is not, of course, a lifestyle choice, but a phase that can sometimes be cruelly and inexplicably fleeting. José Ferrer could vouch for that. The Puerto Rican actor made it big in classic films such as *I Accuse!, Moulin Rouge* and *Cyrano de Bergerac* — for which he won an Oscar — but then, just as he was becoming accustomed to fame and fortune, his agent told him the game was up. 'I'm sorry José, but I can't get any parts for you,' he'd said. 'You're just not hot any more.'

We met in the summer of 1990 when he was about to appear in a play at the Chichester Festival Theatre called *Born Again.* He was then seventy-six and a world-weary soul. He looked back on his life with bemused detachment. 'Let's not beat about the bush,' he said, as I began to delicately inquire about what had happened. 'The truth about José Ferrer is that he made a few good films in the 1950s and then his career went into freefall.'

True, there had been some flashes of the old genius in more recent years — for instance, the sweaty Turkish bey who tried to seduce Peter O'Toole in *Lawrence of Arabia* — but there had also been a lot of embarrassing tosh, such as *The Swarm* and *Dracula's Dog.* 'I'd thought I had a God-given right to a glittering career. It started off so very well and so very effortlessly. I was shocked when it ended so abruptly. I couldn't understand what I'd done wrong and I still can't.'

Some people had suggested his name might have been too 'foreign-sounding' for American audiences, but, then, as he pointed out, if that had been the case, he'd never have made it big in the first place. He could occasionally lose his temper on film sets — 'I only got angry if people weren't behaving professionally,' he said — and others had wondered if maybe he'd been badly advised about his career choices, but actually it was hit after hit until suddenly nothing.

'I think I was just too honest and probably still am. I think if I'd been more inclined to say what was politic, rather than what was on my mind, I'd be a wealthier and more successful man today. Certainly, it isn't ever a good idea if you're an actor to tell a journalist how your career is really going and here I go again.'

Ferrer's confidence had inevitably taken an almighty knock. A possible manifestation of this was a nervous cough, which punctuated virtually every sentence he uttered and sometimes it took him a while to get it under control. It explained why the theatre's publicist had insisted on allocating two hours for the interview, rather than the customary one. After a prolonged attack, I mentioned that I'd never been aware of his cough in his stage and film performances. 'It's funny, really, but I have a much greater degree of confidence when I'm standing before cameras or a live audience. I guess it's because I can shield myself behind a character.'

I asked him how he was getting on with Peter Hall, who was directing him in the play. 'There have been no tantrums, either from me or from him. I need hardly add we've both reached an age when that sort of thing isn't terribly becoming.'

On his fifth and final marriage when I met him and residing mostly in a suburb of Miami, Ferrer said one of the few good things to be said about no longer being a star was that people seldom troubled him for his autograph, which, in his day, he found very irritating. 'I'd be in a

José Ferrer as Captain Dreyfus in *I Accuse* (1958).

hurry to get somewhere and suddenly I'd find myself having to sign endless bits of paper, which I knew would end up soon enough in the dustbin.

'People in the States live forever in the present — if you had a film that came out even a year ago they've already have forgotten about it and you — whereas on this side of the Atlantic there still seems to be a bit of an appetite for the old classics. Still, if anyone ever does remember me, I never quite know what to say — and nor do they. One or two have even blurted out that they thought I'd died.'

José Ferrer was born in Puerto Rico on 8 January 1912, and died in Florida on 26 January 1992, aged eighty.

Geraldine James

After he saw her on Broadway playing Portia to Dustin Hoffman's Shylock in *The Merchant of Venice*, Sam Cohen, the legendary agent, made Geraldine James an offer he imagined she couldn't refuse. 'I did it for Meryl and I can do it for you,' he told her. 'All you will have to do for me is reside in Los Angeles.'

James telephoned Joseph Blatchley, her husband, and told him what Cohen had said and he replied that she'd been away long enough doing her play and it was time to come home. 'The thing is our daughter Ellie had been with me in New York and her fifth birthday was coming up and she was about to start school in England,' James explained. 'My daughter always came first and I got used to my long-time agent saying, when I turned down this or that project because of her, "Oh yes, of course," rather glumly, but it was all about priorities.'

Sir Peter Hall felt that James ranked among the greatest classical actresses. Super-stardom was often there for the taking, only she found it either inconveniencing or requiring her to do work that she felt would be unchallenging. She was criticised for not capitalising more on *The Jewel in the Crown* — one of the most successful television series of the 1980s — but she said the casting directors who got in touch only wanted her to replicate the same kind of role, over and over again, and she couldn't be bothered.

When I met her in 2009, she was about to appear in Howard Barker's play *Victory*, not at a major West End venue, but the respected if tiny Arcola theatre in north-east London. 'I enjoy fringe theatre because you get a real sense of collaboration with the audience which you often don't get in the West End, where, on occasions, you are made uncomfortably aware that people are dozing off,' she said.

Once she had committed to the Arcola — and the inevitably modest stipend they could pay her — she was offered a couple of lucrative, high profile film roles, but, of course, there was no question of her going back on her word. 'I did think "oh God, what have I done?" But I was at least able to accept the role of Mrs Hudson in *Sherlock Holmes* because it was only a small role and I was able to fit it around the play.'

This was not the first time I had interviewed James. I had met her twenty years earlier, when I came away from the encounter with an impression of an angst-ridden young woman who was uneasy in her own skin. She talked to me about how she could not come to terms with the fact her father, a doctor in the Home Counties, had shown her little love during her childhood and left her mother. 'I needed to own up about my early life because it explains why I became an actress. I had to play roles because I did not feel very content about myself as a person. Counselling helped me put that behind me over time. I also managed, towards the end of his life, to come to an accommodation with my father.'

She felt that she had, with the help of her 'beloved rock' of a husband, Joseph, a theatre director and drama teacher, found that elusive state of being called contentment. More than that, she could even laugh at herself. She had a lot of fun, she said, doing the 'Bitty' sketches in *Little Britain*. 'My agent phoned up one day and asked me if I would like to play an over-protective mother. And he added there were some things I needed to know about the part: it involved breast-feeding and the recipient would be a man in his thirties. Of course, I couldn't resist.

'Everybody assumes those breasts were mine, by the way, but in fact they were prosthetic. They were low-slung, which was helpful, because all I had to do was lift a tiny bit of my jersey and David (Walliams) could then pile straight in. There was pipework running through them to provide the necessary liquid and that meant, behind the sofa, there were several men operating a pump.

'I grew fond of those breasts, and, when I was asked to appear in the American version of the series, I asked if I would be getting the same pair and they told me: "No, we have got you Nicole Kidman's." I wasn't sure if that was going to work — Miss Kidman is, after all, a lot thinner than me. I never asked what she had needed them for, but, in the event, they fitted pretty well, so, all in all, I couldn't complain.'

Geraldine James was born in Maidenhead in Berkshire on 6 July 1950.

Tom Wilkinson

om Wilkinson thought he was going to become a star in the mid-eighties when he appeared in a high profile television adaptation of Jeffrey Archer's *First Among Equals*, and then, consolidating his position, he co-starred with Vanessa Redgrave in a highly successful West End production of *Ghosts*. 'After we finished, I took my wife Diana to Bali and imagined I'd have to fight off the job offers when I got back, but I was out of work for months,' he told me. 'It taught me a lesson.'

The year was 1997 and *The Full Monty* had just come out, and there was, once again, talk of Wilkinson becoming a star, but he was understandably not allowing it to go to his head. 'I will tell you something about that first experience. There were all sorts of big parts I imagined I'd get, but, when I saw other actors getting them, I found it rather relaxing as I could say to myself "well, if I'd been doing that, I'd have been so much better". There is a kind of comfort in failure as you don't actually have to prove yourself.'

I was talking to Wilkinson in a coffee shop in north London around the corner from where he lived, and, while the works foreman he played in *The Full Monty* did turn out to be the breakthrough role, the film hadn't been out long enough for him to be recognised. He was a modest, unassuming man, who understood that success in life was ultimately about luck.

He had seen his father, Tom Wilkinson Snr, struggle all his life to bring in an income for his family. 'He was

intelligent and resourceful, but the fates seemed to be against him. When he died, at just fifty, he had debts which amounted to thirty-five pounds. I think he was a man killed by disappointment.' Tom Snr had started out running a small farm in Yorkshire in the late forties, but it was a difficult time and he sold up and moved the family to Canada. 'It was a bold and imaginative step, but once he got us there, he found, even with all his savings, he couldn't afford to buy a farm. He had no alternative but to start work in an aluminium factory, working beside the ovens, which must have been hellish, but he would never beg. Then the market for aluminium began to falter and he brought us back home and got a job as the manager of a pub on Dartmoor. His salary came out of the profits, but these were tiny because the area was so sparsely populated, and he supplemented his income by working as a farm labourer between opening times.'

Wilkinson said he had vivid memories of his father coming home from the farm, taking a bath to wash off the dirt from the fields, and then he would start work in the pub. 'He'd often sit up until closing time with just one customer, nursing a half. He was a quiet man who never complained, but it was inevitable all of this was going to take its toll on his health. I was sixteen when he got seriously ill, and, just before he died, I went to see him lying on his bed and he told me to look after Mum. For him, duty and responsibility were everything, but, after all his hard work, his only legacy was a few bills.'

What Tom Snr never lost was his dignity. Wilkinson seemed touched when I told him how he managed to retain that in Gerald, the part he played in *The Full Monty*. 'I suppose that must have come from my father because I don't believe you can act dignity. We all absorb the things that we see happening to the people we love, so it was inevitable that what happened to my father should, to some extent, have come out in the part I played.'

Wilkinson said that, as he was growing up, it never occurred to him that he would amount to much, but an inspirational head teacher named Molly Sawden raised his horizons. 'I remember when I started at my grammar school in Knaresborough, I had a vague idea that I might end up as a PE teacher or something, but Molly wasn't having any of that. She saw me act and made me think that I might have something to offer. She is very old now, but I value her friendship very much because I realise that, without her, I'd have achieved nothing.'

Still, Wilkinson understood that insecurity was something every actor had to handle in their own way. 'I had a dinner not so long ago with Alec Guinness, when we were making a TV movie together, and I'd imagined after all that he had achieved, he would have the attitude that he could allow himself to rest on his laurels, but I found him every bit as nervous as a young actor starting out, fretting about what he'd be doing next, wondering if his performance would be up to scratch. He set a wonderful example. I mean, if we start to feel that we've made it and we don't have to try any more, we're dead.'

Tom Wilkinson was born in Wharfedale, West Riding of Yorkshire, on 5 February 1948.

Greta Scacchi

You could be forgiven for thinking that before the #MeToo movement began to get traction, men in Hollywood had behaved impeccably towards women. That, as Greta Scacchi knew only too well, was arrant nonsense.

In 2008, when I met her as she was preparing to open in the West End in Terence Rattigan's *The Deep Blue Sea*, she looked back on her time in Hollywood — making films such as *Presumed Innocent* and *Shattered* — with a sense of indignation, if not rage, about what she and other women had to endure. 'I remember going to casting meetings in hotel rooms and there would be all these men looking at me. I went to one with Bill Murray, who asked me for my telephone number in front of everyone and I gave it to him. It was important to show "the team" that there was chemistry between their two putative stars. "Yeah, sure, come over tonight," I said, doing what I was expected to do.

'And, sure enough, Murray came round. I had an eclectic collection of friends in my apartment and we were cooking, playing music, dancing, all completely stoned. He just sat on a sofa, utterly out of his depth. He was wearing his stupid farmer's boots, a lumberjack shirt and looking like the country bumpkin from the Midwest that he really always was. And he left, shaking his head, and I never had to see him again.'

Scacchi also confided how she'd seen Paul Newman — married to Joanne Woodward — in what she called 'a compromising situation', and I agreed to report that only after his death, rather than risk embroiling Scacchi in litigation with the rich and powerful actor.

It might not have been good for her career, but it was good for her soul when she decided to return home to rural Sussex. She could have had the part that made Sharon Stone a star in *Basic Instinct,* but she had no regrets. 'How different it would have been if I had done that film. I imagine they would be paying me ten times more to do this play and there would be a car to come and collect me from some grand hotel and it would have blacked-out windows. I like my life as it is, though. Honestly, I like being able to walk down a street and be left alone. I would have missed out on half of life if I had taken that route.'

Scacchi got to see something of the savageness of man early on in her life when her Italian father hit her. All she'd done was tell him that she wanted to be an actress. He abandoned her mother and her when she was still a child. 'It's telling, I guess, that a lot of the most enduring friendships I have had in my life have been with men who are my father's age — Joss Ackland, for instance, and Michael Blakemore (the director).'

Her relationship with the Hollywood actor Vincent D'Onofrio, the father of her daughter, Leila, also proved to be problematical. She was reluctant to be drawn about it when we met, but she said 'it makes me livid that we are unable to come to an accommodation for the sake of our child'.

Scacchi got to work with some of the biggest names in the acting world, and she was struck by the fact that even Lord Olivier felt self-doubt. They had been making a television drama called *The Ebony Tower*, when they had to do a bedroom scene. She was then twenty-three and he was seventy-eight. His head had been resting against her shoulder and suddenly it felt damp, and, when she looked at him, she realised he had been crying. 'What's wrong?' she asked. He looked back at her despairingly. 'Oh, Greta, I haven't got any more work after this for six months. Nobody wants me any more...'

As Scacchi said: 'Here was this man who was acknowledged as the greatest actor of his day and yet he was riddled with insecurities. I decided there and then that I would never allow myself to get like that. There has to be a point when you can say, "Look, this is who I am — take me or leave me".'

Greta Scacchi was born in Milan on 18 February 1960.

Gwen Ffrangcon-Davies

I've interviewed an actress who played the title role in *Tess of the d'Urbervilles* with the author himself in attendance. Dame Gwen Ffrangcon-Davies was celebrating her ninety-ninth birthday at her little cottage in Stambourne in the Essex countryside when we met and she indubitably still had her wits about her. Always a jobbing actress, she instructed me to make it clear in my piece that she was still very much 'available for work'.

Her old mate Nigel Hawthorne had got in touch to suggest the interview as a birthday treat, and, when I showed up, a television journalist was leaving — Hawthorne had clearly been busy — and the guy looked like the Jolly Green Giant. He'd ruefully explained she'd been chopping parsley with manic intensity as they'd filmed her and it had gone all over his suit.

Ffrangcon-Davies was very much an actress of the Victorian era. She had learnt her craft at the feet of Ellen Terry, Sir Henry Irving's leading lady. Sir John Gielgud, who played Romeo to her Juliet in 1924, considered her to be one of the finest actresses of her generation. In 1950, she succeeded in making the Queen cry when she saw her play Katherine in *Henry VIII* at Stratford. She made only a handful of films — including two Hammer horrors — but she was unforgettable in them. All she could remember of Thomas Hardy, by the way, was that he was a 'respectful and encouraging' presence in the audience, and, when he came backstage afterwards, he told her she was very much how he had envisaged Tess. 'It may well be he was just being polite,' she said.

Ffrangcon-Davies was diminutive, immaculately dressed and made-up, and spoke like a rather fruity Lady Bracknell, a part she once played in a well-regarded stage production. 'I know you journalists like to drink,' she said, and, before I could say a word — it was only 10 a.m. — she poured a very fine amontillado into a pint glass so that it was three-quarters-full. She certainly didn't look her age, but then she never really had. Anna Massey once underestimated it by a quarter of a century. 'I am not old because I do not think of myself as old,' she told me, adamantly. 'And anyway, I can act young.'

She grew to be revered by her peers, but never, for one moment, overtly sought stardom or fame for herself. 'That would have been very vulgar. I have no time for young people who tell me that's what they want. It is something that might happen to you if you are very talented and very lucky, but it should be the last thing on your mind when you are starting out. My dear, the presumption.'

In her long career, she had, in any case, seen how many couldn't cope with it. 'Sometimes they achieve it all too

early and it's too much. Sometimes it proves to be a transient quality. Others, of course, just haven't the temperament for it and it's terribly damaging, and, in this unhappy regard, I think of poor dear Vivien Leigh.' She said, however, that one of the great pleasures of being around for a very long time was seeing people who, when they were starting out, she might have dismissed as 'quite mediocre', but, in old age, they sometimes ripened into something 'unexpectedly impressive.' Ffrangcon-Davies was, by contrast, good and dependable throughout her career.

Not long before we'd met, I had seen her on the *Wogan* chat show, when she had recited, word for word and very movingly, Juliet's death scene. 'Oh, no one can make a mess of Shakespeare,' she'd said when I mentioned it. She made her final acting appearance in a teleplay of the Sherlock Holmes mystery *The Master Blackmailer* at the age of 100. 'You don't retire, unless you have to,' she told me. 'Who wants to be left twiddling their thumbs between giving up a job they love and the grave?'

Dame Gwen Ffrangcon-Davies was born on 25 January 1891, in London, and died in Halstead, Essex, on 27 January 1992, at the age of 101.

Antonia de Sancha

I used to receive a document each week called *The Celebrity Bulletin*, which was a kind of lonely hearts column that brought together visiting stars seeking publicity with native journalists who needed to fill space. There was naturally an imperative on Robert Maxwell's *European* to finding stars who had good European credentials, and that — and I suppose cognitive dissonance — was how I alighted upon a Spanish actress named Antonia de Sancha.

The Bulletin announced that Miss de Sancha had jetted into London to appear in *Alien III* that was in production at Pinewood Studios with Sigourney Weaver in the leading role. Although I hadn't heard of her, I immediately telephoned the contact number listed and asked a man at the other end of the line if I could take Miss de Sancha to lunch at Le Caprice and talk to her about her life and career, and could she also please find the time in her busy schedule to pose for my photographer, Graham Trott? The man sounded distracted — there was a woman talking in the background — but all was sorted in a matter of minutes.

I mentioned at morning conference that I had Miss de Sancha in mind as the big picture story for my page and Ian Watson, the editor, raised a quizzical eyebrow. He said he'd never heard of her. I said it was my belief that she was very big in Spain, and, besides, she was about to co-star with Sigourney Weaver in *Alien III*. I then called Graham

Antonia de Sancha with her publicist, Max Clifford (left). Clifford died in prison serving an eight-year sentence for multiple counts of indecent assault.

who also said he'd never heard of her, but very well, he'd do the picture. I asked Jesus Adorno, the maître d' of Le Caprice, if Miss de Sancha and I could have the coveted corner table in his restaurant, and, while he hadn't heard of her, either, it looked like they were short of stars that day so he gave in.

So there was I early in January 1991 sitting at the corner table of Le Caprice waiting for Miss de Sancha to make her grand entrance. That she eventually did so forty minutes late only made me even more certain she had to be a star who resided in the highest possible place in the firmament. Even Lauren Bacall, when I had lunched with her at the same restaurant, arrived only ten minutes after the appointed hour.

In person, Miss de Sancha was breathless, and, I have to say, a bit sweaty. 'I'm awfully sorry,' she said. 'You must forgive me.' I graciously told her to think nothing of it, ordered two glasses of champagne and solicitously inquired if perhaps a scene she was doing with Miss

Weaver and/or the third alien had overrun. 'There's bad news on that front, I'm afraid,' she said. 'The part I had in the film was edited out at a last-minute script conference. This sort of thing happens a lot in film-making and you just have to get used to it.'

She was twenty-four, attractive in her own kind of way, if not especially polished, and we ended up having what felt like a very studenty conversation about the highs and lows of life as a struggling actress. It became clear that, so far from jetting into London, she'd lived in the city all her life. I established, however, that her father was definitely Spanish, even if her mother was Swedish. I asked her to talk through her career and there wasn't a lot to say. 'Only there was this guy who was auditioning with me at the Royal Academy of Dramatic Art, and he was really into interpretative acting, and, while he was doing an erotic scene, he actually took his trousers down in front of the examiners as he spoke his lines. The members of the panel were pretty old and had seen everything and they didn't say a word, but they failed him, needless to say.'

I persevered and got a long monologue about how acting is such dreadful hard work, it's so difficult to get any good scripts, but she couldn't ever countenance doing anything else. On how far things had developed with *Alien III* and Sigourney Weaver she was at best evasive.

I did what I could with the interview when I wrote it up, which was to say not a lot, but we used it big because Graham's photograph of her was terrific. I thought nothing more of the encounter until late one night a year later when I started getting calls from other journalists asking me what I'd made of her. One of them even asked me how 'close' I had been to Miss de Sancha and another expressed surprise that I'd felt the need to interview her when no other journalist ever had. It turned out she had gone on to have an affair with the cabinet minister David

Mellor that contributed to the end of his marriage and his departure from John Major's government.

Graham ended up making a fortune out of the picture he'd reluctantly taken of Miss de Sancha, I got a ticking off from my editor for not keeping in touch with her, and the woman herself found, on all those front pages, a fleeting kind of stardom. She was last heard of working in a shop in Notting Hill.

Antonia de Sancha was born in Hammersmith on 14 September 1961.

Antonia de Sancha poses with Max Clifford.

INDEX

Image Credits

115. Press Association
116. Press Association
123. BBC
126. RKO Pictures
129. Century 21 Productions
131. Century 21 Productions
137. BBC
138. National Theatre
142. Yash Raj Films
145. ITV
150. BBC
152. Royal Academy of Arts
154. New York Times
155. The Times
163. Royal Mail
164. BBC
169. The Daily Telegraph
170. BBC
172. ITV
179. Paramount Pictures
182. Columbia Pictures
185. TriStar Pictures
186. MGM
191. United Artists
192. Universal Pictures
197. 20th Century Fox
202. BBC
205. National Portrait Gallery
207. Reuters
213. ITV
216. ITV
219. Peter Hapak/ New York Magazine
223. Associated British-Pathé
227. MGM
241. The Guardian

Acknowledgements

It was Terry Page, when he was editor of the *Evening Argus* in Brighton in the mid-eighties, who laid the foundation stone for *Star Turns*. He agreed to let me have a regular slot in his paper, interviewing famous people who were associated with Sussex. The *Argus Interview* won me Young Journalist of the Year in the British Press Awards, and, thanks to the late Anthony Howard, my first job in national newspapers on *The Observer*. I doubt my career could have happened without them, or, for that matter, W M Hill and Ray Horsfield, respectively the editor and news editor of the *Evening Echo* in Bournemouth, who saw something in an otherwise unemployable teenager just out of school and gave me my first job in newspapers.

I owe Mat Kelly, the founder of *The New European*, too, for giving me a new lease of professional life, and Jasper Copping, its editor, for agreeing to *Star Turns* beginning life as a series in the paper to enable me to retain my theatre review slot when the pandemic made theatre reviewing impossible. Sincere thanks, too, to Richard Nelsson — Guardian News & Media's charming and indefatigable Information Manager — for helping me to disinter some of my earliest cuttings. Thanks also to Julia Braybrook, Nick Robinson, Richard Pendlebury, Richard Eden, Richard Brooks, Ian Walker and Simon Nayyar, as well, of course, as Malcolm Turner and Gurdeep Mattu at SunRise Publishing for giving a lazy old hack the kick up the backside he needed to write another book.

Tim Walker, London, July 2021.